Upgrade
your French

Upgrade
your French

Margaret Jubb

UNIVERSITY OF ABERDEEN

A member of the
Hodder Headline Group
LONDON
Co-published in the United States of America by
Oxford University Press Inc., New York

First published in Great Britain in 2002 by
Arnold, a member of the Hodder Headline Group,
338 Euston Road, London NW1 3BH

http://www.arnoldpublishers.com

Co-published in the United States of America by
Oxford University Press Inc.,
198 Madison Avenue, New York, NY10016

British Library Cataloguing in Publication Data
A catalogue record for this book is available from the British Library

Library of Congress Cataloging-in-Publication Data
A catalog record for this book is available from the Library of Congress

ISBN 0 340 76345 0 (pb)

2 3 4 5 6 7 8 9 10

Production Editor: Rada Radojicic
Production Controller: Bryan Eccleshall
Cover Design: Terry Griffiths
Illustrations: Colin Wheeler

Typeset in 10/12 pt Formata by Cambrian Typesetters, Frimley, Surrey
Printed and bound in Malta by Gutenberg Press

What do you think about this book? Or any other Arnold title?
Please send your comments to feedback.arnold@hodder.co.uk

Contents

Acknowledgements

My first thanks are to Elena Seymenliyska, Arnold's Commissioning Editor for Modern Languages, who invited me to write this book, and who has been an invaluable source of advice and support throughout. I am also indebted to my students in the French Department at Aberdeen University, who have worked through my material in its various drafts and have helped to make it more user-friendly. Last, but by no means least, I should like to thank Jennifer Bellanger and Isabelle Gourdin for the care with which they have checked the whole text, and John Roach for his help in resolving a number of troublesome queries. For any remaining inaccuracies and infelicities, I am of course entirely responsible.

Margaret Jubb

The author and publisher would like to thank the following for permission to use copyright material in this book: Presses Universitaires de France: *Cahiers Internationaux de Sociologie,* LXXX (1986), p. 149.

Introduction

AIMS OF THE BOOK

If you are likely to get very high marks in your French language examinations, this book is not for you. It is not aimed at high-flyers, but at students in all years of their degree programmes who need to improve their performance. It offers you a thirty-day revision and consolidation course to work through on your own with exercises that will take between half an hour and an hour per day. If you follow it conscientiously, you will improve your level of performance significantly, hence the title, *Upgrade your French.*

It is not realistic to expect to learn very complex and subtle aspects of the French language for the first time just before examinations and when you are working on your own. Instead, this book focuses on three key areas where you can make a real difference:

- spotting mistakes and correcting errors/oversights on key grammar points;
- making a conscious effort to improve the style of your French;
- making a conscious effort to use more adventurous vocabulary and avoid Anglicisms.

In order to maintain interest and concentration, a day spent working on a key grammar point is followed typically by a day focusing more on matters of style or vocabulary, though grammar can rarely be avoided entirely! In fact, consolidation of the previous day's work has been deliberately built into the programme, so ideally you should follow the order of the book in order to gain the maximum benefit from it.

GETTING THE MOST FROM THIS BOOK

The idea is to complete one unit per day over a period of thirty days. You will find that you absorb the material better if you work steadily in this way, rather than trying to race ahead and do two or three units per day. If you want to do more language revision each day, then vary your activities by doing some other work of your own, e.g. going over vocabulary lists, revising verbs, looking over corrected work, working on past papers, or, perhaps best of all, reading a French newspaper or book.

Each day's work from this book should take you no more than an hour. If you find you haven't finished in that time, it's probably better to stop anyway and go back to it later when you feel refreshed. When you have finished, check your work against the answer key at the back of the book, and count your total of correct answers out of 30. If you have full marks, well done. If you got less than 20/30, you should do the section again, but not immediately. Give yourself at least an hour before going back to it. If you got between 20 and 29 out of 30, you should look back at where you went wrong the next day before you move on to the following section. Make sure you understand why you went wrong before you do move on.

As well as doing the exercises and checking your answers, you should note down as you work through each section any vocabulary or idioms which were unfamiliar to you. Always list nouns with their gender and verbs with their irregularities and dependent prepositions (where applicable). You should also use the references to grammar books given at the end of each section to look up any points on which you need fuller explanation. The brief explanations given in this book do not aim to give exhaustive coverage. They focus instead on points which are known from experience to cause many students recurrent problems. Experience was reinforced in this case by the analysis of a sizeable sample of past students' examination papers. You will find that some of the errors from the sample have been included in the book as exercise material for you to correct.

The most important thing, though, is that you learn to correct your own work. You will know more precisely when you have finished working through *Upgrade your French*, if you don't know already, where your major problems arise. Bear all this in mind and if you know, for example, that in a stressful examination situation, or even when writing under less pressure, you are liable to miss adjective agreements, then try to leave time to check your written work specifically for this.

APPLYING WHAT YOU HAVE LEARNT

Time permitting, it is always a good idea to check your work over a number of times, looking separately each time for a particular feature, e.g.

- checking the gender of all the nouns;
- use of articles;
- checking all the adjectives/past participles for agreement;
- checking all the verbs for correct tense, formation and agreement with the subject;
- checking the pronouns (direct/indirect object);
- checking all the relative pronouns;
- checking the verb constructions (active/passive) and use of prepositions where applicable.

You can expand/contract this list to suit your particular needs. Pay particular attention to checking the last few sentences of your work where flagging concentration can cause slips to occur. You should find that methodical checking in this way enables you to remedy many errors for yourself and to avoid losing marks unnecessarily for things which you have overlooked in the heat of the moment.

You should also be conscious of matters of vocabulary, both as you write and when you are doing your checking at the end. So, for example, you could be on the lookout for obvious Anglicisms of vocabulary, such as misuse of **issue** (see Day 10). You could also check for overuse of one item of very basic vocabulary, e.g. **dire** in a passage of reported speech (see Day 2), and aim for more variety.

Style is something to be conscious of as you write, rather than when you have finished and it is too late to change. Don't be so afraid of losing marks by making errors that you limit yourself to monotonously simple and safe constructions. You can be sure that you will gain marks for being adventurous, even if occasionally the grammar does go a little astray in the process. So, think about varying your sentence openings (see Day 24), ring the changes on boring **et** and **mais** (see Day 22) and try using some inversions of verb and subject (see Day 19). If you do all this, your marks are bound to improve. Good luck!

As in English, verbs in French agree with their subject in number (singular/plural) and person. This may seem a very obvious elementary point, but it is one which is all too easily overlooked when you are under pressure in an exam. It is important first of all to remember that many French verb forms which sound the same as one another are written differently.

I First-/third-person singular

Pay careful attention to the difference between first-person and third-person singular endings, for example, in the present tense (see also Day 3) of regular **-ir** verbs (**je finis**, **il finit**), semi-regular **-ir** verbs (**je dors**, **il dort**), **-re** verbs (**j'attends**, **il attend**) and irregular verbs (**je peux**, **il peut**), and in the imperfect and conditional tenses of all verbs (**j'avais**, **il avait**; **j'aurais**, **il aurait**). Watch **avoir** and **être** particularly, since they occur so frequently, being used to form compound tenses of other verbs.

Complete the sentences below with the verbs in the appropriate form of the present tense.

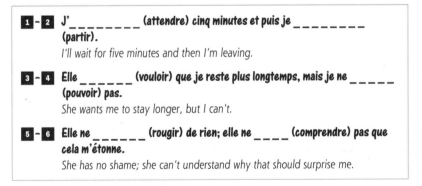

1 - 2 J'_____ (attendre) cinq minutes et puis je _____ (partir).
I'll wait for five minutes and then I'm leaving.

3 - 4 Elle _____ (vouloir) que je reste plus longtemps, mais je ne _____ (pouvoir) pas.
She wants me to stay longer, but I can't.

5 - 6 Elle ne _____ (rougir) de rien; elle ne ____ (comprendre) pas que cela m'étonne.
She has no shame; she can't understand why that should surprise me.

Rewrite the sentences below in the first person singular.

7 - 8 Quand elle était plus jeune, elle avait les cheveux longs.
When she was younger, she had long hair.

9 - 10 S'il avait pris le train de 9 heures il y serait arrivé à temps.
If he had caught the 9 o'clock train, he would have got there in time.

II Third-person singular/plural

The distinction between third-person singular and plural endings also requires partic-ular attention, because in many cases the two forms sound the same. It is easy to make a mistake when the verb is some distance away from its subject, particularly if another noun intervenes. For example:

Le taux d'inflation dans ces pays varie énormément.
[The inflation rate in these countries varies enormously.]

Be particularly careful with relative clauses. Make sure that the verb in the relative clause agrees with the subject of the relative clause and not with the subject of the main clause. For example:

La petite avait des parents qui travaillaient toute la journée.
[The little girl's parents worked all day.]

Note that mistakes are frequently made with with the present tense of **-er** verbs (**varie/varient**) and with the third-person singular/plural endings of the imperfect and conditional tenses (**-ait/-aient**).

Complete the sentences below with the verb in the third-person singular or plural form as appropriate.

> **11**   *La qualité de ces produits _ _ _ _ _ (être) tout à fait exceptionnelle.*
> *The quality of these products is quite outstanding.*
>
> **12**   *Elle aimait lire des romans qui la _ _ _ _ _ _ (faire) rêver.*
> *She liked to read novels which made her dream.*

As a final note on this point, watch out for nouns which are plural in French but whose equivalent in English is singular (or vice versa) and make sure that the verb agrees appropriately. For example:

Les informations passent à vingt heures.
[The news is on at 8 p.m.]
Ses recherches portent sur les complications de l'hypertension.
[His/her research is concerned with the complications of high blood pressure.]
Son pantalon fait des poches aux genoux.
[His/her trousers are baggy at the knees.]

Complete the following sentences with the appropriate form of the verbs given.

> **13**   *Ce pantalon vous _ _ _ _ (aller) très bien.*
> *Those trousers suit you very well.*
>
> **14**   *Les renseignements fournis dans le texte _ _ _ _ (être) inexacts.*
> *The information given in the text is inaccurate.*

III Two or more subjects linked by *et*

Where one verb has two or more individual subjects, remember to make the verb plural. For example:

> **Le Président et le Premier Ministre se sont rencontrés hier.**
> [The President and the Prime Minister met yesterday.]
> **L'introduction et la conclusion sont à refaire.**
> [The introduction and conclusion will have to be rewritten.]

Be especially careful where a first-person subject is combined with a third-person; the verb must be first-person plural. For example:

> **Mon ami et moi partons en vacances demain.**
> [My boyfriend and I are leaving on holiday tomorrow.]

Complete the following sentences with the verbs in the appropriate present tense form.

---

15 **L'écrivain et sa femme _ _ _ _ _ _ _ _ (aller) collaborer à la production de ce film.**
The writer and his wife are going to collaborate on the production of this film.

16 **Son intelligence et sa perspicacité _ _ _ _ _ _ _ (être) vraiment remarquables.**
His intelligence and insight are truly remarkable.

17 **La France et l'Allemagne _ _ _ _ _ _ _ _ _ _ (se rapprocher).**
France and Germany are beginning to enjoy better relations.

18 **Mes parents et moi _ _ _ _ _ _ _ _ (aller) assister au mariage.**
My parents and I are going to attend the wedding.

IV Impersonal verbs

Remember that if you are using verbs such as **exister, manquer, rester** or **se trouver** impersonally, the verb must be third-person singular. Contrast the following impersonal and personal uses of these verbs:

Il manque deux dossiers.	**Deux dossiers manquent.**
[Two files are missing.]	
Il existe plusieurs modèles.	**Plusieurs modèles existent.**
[Several styles are available.]	

English speakers often try to use the impersonal verb **il s'agit de** with a personal subject. e.g. to translate 'this book is about . . .' they use ***ce livre s'agit de . . .** This is an impossible construction and must never be attempted. Always use this verb in the third person singular with impersonal **il** as its subject. For example:

> **Dans ce livre il s'agit de . . .**
> [This book is about . . .]

Dans ces articles il s'agit de . . .
[These articles are about . . .]

Rewrite the following sentences using the impersonal verb indicated.

---

19 **Deux parts de gâteau restent. (rester)**
Two pieces of cake are left.

20 **Tous ces films traitent à peu près de la même histoire. (s'agir)**
All these films deal with more or less the same story.

V   Problems with collective nouns

Thinking in English is the great danger here. Whereas singular collective nouns, such as council, family or government, may take either a singular or plural verb in English, in French there is no choice; they must take a singular verb. For example:

Le gouvernement a décidé d'introduire un nouveau projet de loi.
[The government has/have decided to introduce a new bill.]

You should note, however, that the situation is different if the collective noun in French is followed by **de** + plural. In such a case, the verb may be singular or plural, but is more usually plural. For example:

Un groupe d'étudiants attendaient (or attendait) devant la porte.
[A group of students was/were waiting outside the door.]

There is no choice with **tout le monde**; you must always use a singular verb. For example:

Tout le monde s'accorde à reconnaître la justesse de cette décision.
[Everyone acknowledges that this decision is correct.]

Decide whether the verb in the following sentences should be singular or plural.

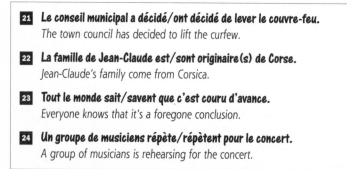

21 **Le conseil municipal a décidé/ont décidé de lever le couvre-feu.**
The town council has decided to lift the curfew.

22 **La famille de Jean-Claude est/sont originaire(s) de Corse.**
Jean-Claude's family come from Corsica.

23 **Tout le monde sait/savent que c'est couru d'avance.**
Everyone knows that it's a foregone conclusion.

24 **Un groupe de musiciens répète/répètent pour le concert.**
A group of musicians is rehearsing for the concert.

VI Quantifiers

The usual pattern is for **la plupart, (un grand) nombre de, beaucoup de** to take a plural verb, agreeing with the usually plural complement. For example:

La plupart des étudiants ont réussi à leur examen.

[Most of the students have passed their exam.]

But occasionally, if a singular complement is involved, a singular verb will be needed. For example:

La plupart de la cathédrale a été reconstruite.

[Most of the cathedral has been rebuilt.]

Fractions, such as **la moitié**, when they are followed by a plural complement, take a plural verb. For example:

La moitié des étudiants ont échoué.

[Half the students have failed.]

But if the complement is singular, the verb will also be singular. For example:

La moitié de la classe était absente.

[Half the class was absent.]

Percentages are usually followed by a plural verb. For example:

33% des mariages se terminent par le divorce.

[33% of marriages end in divorce.]

Decide whether the verb in the following sentences should be singular or plural.

---

25 **La moitié des étudiants s'est inscrite/se sont inscrits une semaine à l'avance.**
Half the students registered a week in advance.

26 **La plupart des Hollandais parle/parlent plus d'une langue.**
Most Dutch people speak more than one language.

27 **60% des professeurs se déclare satisfait/se déclarent satisfaits de leurs conditions de travail.**
60% of teachers say that they are happy with their working conditions.

28 **La moitié de la classe a/ont échoué.**
Half the class has failed.

29 **Beaucoup de ses livres est/sont illisible(s).**
Many of his/her books are unreadable.

VII   Agreement with *être*

In careful French, where **ce** is followed by a third-person plural complement, the verb **être** is supposed to be third-person plural. For example:

> **Ce sont les femmes qui doivent en être responsables.**
> [It's women who have to take responsibility.]

For once you don't need to worry unduly about this! You will find and you will get away with **c'est** followed by a plural complement, *but* you must make sure that the verb in the relative clause agrees in person and number with the complement. For example:

> **C'est moi qui le dis.**
> [*I'm* (italics for emphasis) telling you so.]
> **C'est vous qui devez y aller.**
> [*You* have to go there.]
> **C'est nous qui faisons les courses.**
> [*We* do the shopping.]

Complete the following sentence with the verb in the appropriate form.

---

30   *C'est moi qui (faire) la cuisine.*
     I do the cooking.

See for further information
Hawkins and Towell, 9.1–9.1.6
Byrne and Churchill, §§337, 390–7
Ferrar, §62

Upgrade your style: Reporting speech

I   Reported speech

*There is a very wide range of verbs in French which can be used to report speech and thoughts and if you make a conscious effort to ring the changes on overused verbs such as **dire**, **penser** and **répondre**, you can make an immediate improvement to your style.*

The following is just a small selection of verbs which you should include in your active vocabulary.

affirmer, **maintenir** to claim, maintain	**constater**, **noter**, **observer**, **indiquer** to note, observe, indicate
annoncer, **déclarer** to announce, declare	
ajouter, **préciser** to add	**expliquer**, **exposer** to explain, outline
assurer to assure	
admettre, **avouer**, **reconnaître**, **révéler** to admit, reveal	**faire remarquer**, **signaler** to point out
considérer, **estimer**, **être de l'avis que**, **trouver** to think	**répliquer**, **rétorquer**, **riposter** to retort

Complete the following sentences by filling in the blanks with an appropriate verb from the list above. This exercise has been designed to consolidate the work which you did in Day 1 on agreement of verb and subject, so pay particular attention to the endings of your verbs!

---

1   La plupart des députés _ _ _ _ _ _ _ _ _ _ _ que ces mesures sont insuffisantes.
Most MPs think that these measures are inadequate.

2   Mon mari et moi _ _ _ _ _ _ _ _ _ _ _ _ _ _ qu'il y avait eu une erreur.
My husband and I pointed out that there had been a mistake.

3   Beaucoup d'étudiants _ _ _ _ _ _ _ _ _ _ _ _ _ _ _ qu'ils n'avaient pas lu le livre.
A lot of students admitted that they had not read the book.

4   Le gouvernement _ _ _ _ _ _ _ _ _ _ _ que le référendum serait remis à plus tard.
The government declared that the referendum would be postponed.

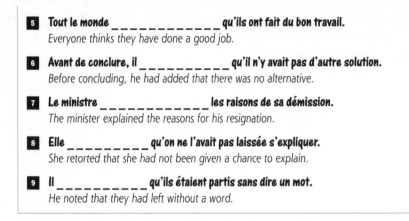

5 **Tout le monde** _ _ _ _ _ _ _ _ _ _ _ _ _ **qu'ils ont fait du bon travail.**
Everyone thinks they have done a good job.

6 **Avant de conclure, il** _ _ _ _ _ _ _ _ _ _ **qu'il n'y avait pas d'autre solution.**
Before concluding, he had added that there was no alternative.

7 **Le ministre** _ _ _ _ _ _ _ _ _ _ _ _ **les raisons de sa démission.**
The minister explained the reasons for his resignation.

8 **Elle** _ _ _ _ _ _ _ _ _ _ **qu'on ne l'avait pas laissée s'expliquer.**
She retorted that she had not been given a chance to explain.

9 **Il** _ _ _ _ _ _ _ _ _ _ _ **qu'ils étaient partis sans dire un mot.**
He noted that they had left without a word.

II   Use of tenses in reported speech

Remember to pay particular attention to the use of tenses in reported speech when the reporting verb is in the past (passé composé, past historic, pluperfect). The following changes will occur:

Direct speech	Reported speech
Elle est (present)	**Elle était** (imperfect)
Elle sera (future) **Elle aura été** (future perfect)	**Elle serait** (conditional) **Elle aurait été** (past conditional)
Elle a été (passé composé)	**Elle avait été** (pluperfect)

Study the following examples by way of illustration and note the change of pronouns as well as the change of tenses in the second and fourth examples.

> **«Elle est à Paris.» Il a dit qu'elle était à Paris.**
> ['She is in Paris.' He said that she was in Paris.]
> **«Je serai contente.» Elle a dit qu'elle serait contente.**
> ['I will be pleased.' She said that she would be pleased.]
> **«Elle aura été étonnée.» Il a dit qu'elle aurait été étonnée.**
> ['She will have been amazed.' He said that she would have been amazed.]
> **«J'ai été contente.» Elle a dit qu'elle avait été contente.**
> ['I was pleased.' She said that she had been pleased.]

Rewrite the following sentences as reported speech, making any necessary changes to pronouns as well as to verb tenses. Introduce the speech with the verb indicated in brackets at the end. Give an English translation of each of these verbs and look back at Section I above to check if necessary.

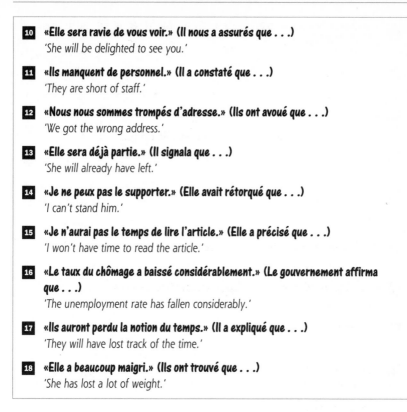

10 «Elle sera ravie de vous voir.» (Il nous a assurés que . . .)
'She will be delighted to see you.'

11 «Ils manquent de personnel.» (Il a constaté que . . .)
'They are short of staff.'

12 «Nous nous sommes trompés d'adresse.» (Ils ont avoué que . . .)
'We got the wrong address.'

13 «Elle sera déjà partie.» (Il signala que . . .)
'She will already have left.'

14 «Je ne peux pas le supporter.» (Elle avait rétorqué que . . .)
'I can't stand him.'

15 «Je n'aurai pas le temps de lire l'article.» (Elle a précisé que . . .)
'I won't have time to read the article.'

16 «Le taux du chômage a baissé considérablement.» (Le gouvernement affirma que . . .)
'The unemployment rate has fallen considerably.'

17 «Ils auront perdu la notion du temps.» (Il a expliqué que . . .)
'They will have lost track of the time.'

18 «Elle a beaucoup maigri.» (Ils ont trouvé que . . .)
'She has lost a lot of weight.'

III   Use of the conditional/past conditional for unconfirmed reports

The conditional and past conditional are often used in the media for unconfirmed reports. For example:

> **Il y aurait une vingtaine de blessés.**
> [There may be some twenty people injured.]
> **Il serait mort à l'hôpital.**
> [Apparently he died in hospital.]

As you will see from these examples, the conditional is used where a present tense would be used in a straightforward statement of fact, and the past conditional is used instead of a past historic/passé composé or pluperfect. You can imitate this usage yourself if you are reporting a statement/allegation which is not your own. It is often useful to introduce such statements with **D'après**, **Selon**, or **A en croire**, all of which mean 'according to'. For example:

> **D'après *Le Figaro*, il n'y aurait aucun espoir de réussite.**
> [According to *Le Figaro*, there is no hope of success.]

Selon un porte-parole, le Premier Ministre se serait déjà décidé à démissionner.
[According to a spokesperson, the Prime Minister has already decided to resign.]

In other contexts, you may use the verb **prétendre que** (to claim that). For example:

Il a prétendu que son frère lui aurait donné l'argent.
[He claimed that his brother had given him the money.]

Rewrite the following sentences, introducing the statements as indicated, and making clear by your choice of tenses that you do not personally vouch for the truth of what is said.

---

19   **Il est malade depuis trois jours. (D'après sa secrétaire, . . .)**
He has been ill for three days. (According to his secretary, . . .)

20   **On lui a donné de violents coups de pieds. (Selon les témoins, . . .)**
He was violently kicked. (According to the witnesses, . . .)

21   **Il s'agit d'un incendie criminel. (D'après la police . . .)**
It's a case of an arson attack. (According to the police, . . .)

22   **Tout s'est bien passé. (A en croire le rapport, . . .)**
Everything went well. (According to the report/If the report is to be believed, . . .)

23   **Il avait été malade. (Il a prétendu que . . .)**
He had been ill. (He claimed that . . .)

24   **Son frère lui avait volé l'argent. (Il a prétendu que . . .)**
His brother had stolen the money from him. (He claimed that . . .)

IV   Inversion of subject and verb after direct speech
Finally, remember that following a passage of direct speech, you need to place the subject after the verb of saying. For example:

«Je n'ai aucune idée», répondit-elle.
['I have no idea,' she replied.]
«Vous le trouverez à votre gauche», dit le guide.
['You will find it on your left,' the guide said/said the guide.]

This second example illustrates the difference between English and French. In English, we have the option of placing a noun subject after the verb, but we can equally well place it before the verb. In French there is no such choice.

Correct the errors in the following sentences.

25 «Si seulement je l'avais su!» elle s'est écriée.
'If only I had known!' she exclaimed.

26 «Je partirai mardi», Sophie précisa.
'I will be leaving on Tuesday,' Sophie added.

27 «Pourriez-vous me donner un coup de main?», ma voisine m'a demandé.
'Could you give me a hand?' my neighbour asked.

28 «Est-ce que j'ai le temps de prendre un café?» elle s'est demandé.
'Have I got time for a cup of coffee?' she wondered.

Remember that if the verb of saying comes in the middle of a passage of direct speech, you still need to place the subject after the verb. For example:

> **«Avant d'aller à l'aéroport,» expliqua-t-il, «je dois passer à la banque.»**
> ['Before I go to the airport,' he explained, 'I have to call in at the bank.']

Correct the errors in the following sentences.

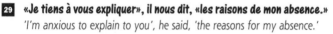

29 «Je tiens à vous expliquer», il nous dit, «les raisons de mon absence.»
'I'm anxious to explain to you', he said, 'the reasons for my absence.'

30 «Cela», le professeur observa, «est un vrai mystère.»
'That', the teacher said, 'is a real mystery.'

See for further information
Hawkins and Towell, Chapter 10
Jubb and Rouxeville, Chapters 3, 4, 6, 7
Byrne and Churchill, §§415–17
Ferrar, §63
See also Day 6 for adverbs of manner.

Key points: The present tense

The present tense is the one which has the most irregularities and so understandably students often make mistakes with it. You may need to revise its formation in a reference grammar book (see page references given at the end of this unit) before you attempt the exercises which follow. The comments and exercises here focus on some common problems rather than attempting coverage of all the irregularities.

I Regular -er verbs

The stem is found by removing the **-er** of the infinitive. Problems often arise with the following:

- Verbs whose stem ends in a vowel, e.g. **étudier**, **remercier**. Be careful not to omit the final vowel of the stem. Distinguish between the noun **étude** and the verb forms, **j'étud*i*e**, **il étud*i*e**, etc.
- Verbs whose stem ends in **-d** or **-t**, e.g. **accorder**, **présenter**. Be careful not to omit the ending of the verb. Distinguish between the nouns **accord**, **présent** and the verb forms **il accorde**, **il présente**, and don't confuse these **-er** verbs with **-ir** or **-re** verbs which do end in **-d** or **-t** in the third-person singular, e.g. **il attend** (infinitive **attendre**), **il part** (infinitive **partir**).
- Always be on your guard to distinguish between a noun and a verb, e.g. **le travail**, but **il travaille**.

Complete the sentences below with the correct form of the present tense.

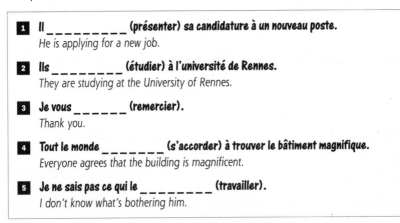

1 Il _ _ _ _ _ _ _ _ _ _ (présenter) sa candidature à un nouveau poste.
He is applying for a new job.

2 Ils _ _ _ _ _ _ _ _ (étudier) à l'université de Rennes.
They are studying at the University of Rennes.

3 Je vous _ _ _ _ _ _ (remercier).
Thank you.

4 Tout le monde _ _ _ _ _ _ _ _ (s'accorder) à trouver le bâtiment magnifique.
Everyone agrees that the building is magnificent.

5 Je ne sais pas ce qui le _ _ _ _ _ _ _ _ _ (travailler).
I don't know what's bothering him.

II   Semi-regular -er verbs

The stems of some **-er** verbs change their form when they are followed by a mute **e**, i.e. in all the singular forms and in the third-person plural of the present tense.

- Most verbs ending in **-eler** or **-eter** double the final consonant of the stem. For example:
  appeler: j'appelle, tu appelles, il appelle, ils appellent, but **nous appelons, vous appelez**
  jeter: je jette, tu jettes, il jette, ils jettent, but **nous jetons, vous jetez**
- As a variant on the above, some verbs change the first **e** to **è**. For example:
  acheter: j'achète, tu achètes, il achète, ils achètent, but **nous achetons, vous achetez**
- Some verbs ending in **-ener** behave likewise. For example:
  mener: je mène, tu mènes, il mène, ils mènent, but **nous menons, vous menez**
- Accent changes occur to verbs ending in **-é** + consonant + **er**. For example:
  céder: je cède, tu cèdes, il cède, ils cèdent, but **nous cédons, vous cédez**
  espérer: j'espère, tu espères, il espère, ils espèrent, but **nous espérons, vous espérez**
- Verbs whose stem ends in **-y** change the **y** to **i**. For example:
  essayer: j'essaie, tu essaies, il essaie, ils essaient, but **nous essayons, vous essayez**
- Finally, there is a spelling change to note in the first person plural of verbs in **-cer, -ger**. This occurs in order to preserve the soft sound of the **c** or **g** before **o**. For example:
  nous commençons, nous mangeons.

Complete the sentences below with the correct form of the present tense.

---

6   Ils _ _ _ _ _ _ _ (mener) une vie très mouvementée.
They lead a very hectic life.

7   Ils ne _ _ _ _ _ _ _ (jeter) jamais rien.
They never throw anything away.

8   Elle _ _ _ _ _ _ _ _ (employer) les grands moyens pour arriver à ses fins.
She resorts to drastic measures to achieve her ends.

9   Je _ _ _ _ _ _ _ _ _ (préférer) le café au thé.
I prefer coffee to tea.

10   Quand il fait mauvais nous nous _ _ _ _ _ _ _ _ (plonger) dans la lecture.
When the weather is bad we bury ourselves in our books.

III   Regular and semi-regular -ir verbs

Watch the difference between the first/second-person singular endings and the third-person singular (see Day 1, Section I). For example: **je finis, tu finis, il finit**; **je pars, tu pars, il part**.

Perhaps the most common problem is forgetting to put the **-ss** 'infix' between the stem and the endings in the plural of regular **-ir** verbs. For example: **nous choisissons, vous choisissez, ils choisissent.** There is no infix, though, with semi-regular verbs. For example: **nous dormons, vous dormez, ils dorment**.

You find the stem for the singular of semi-regular **-ir** verbs, e.g. **partir** by taking the infinitive and removing not just the **-ir** but the previous consonant as well, giving the stem **par-** and the verb forms **je pars, tu pars, il part**. Be careful not to use the present subjunctive form, **je parte**, by accident.

Correct the errors in the following sentences written by students.

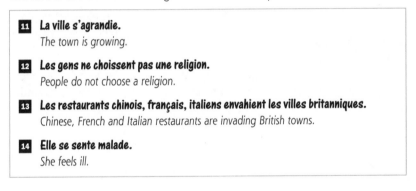

11   **La ville s'agrandie.**
   The town is growing.

12   **Les gens ne choissent pas une religion.**
   People do not choose a religion.

13   **Les restaurants chinois, français, italiens envahient les villes britanniques.**
   Chinese, French and Italian restaurants are invading British towns.

14   **Elle se sente malade.**
   She feels ill.

IV   Regular -re verbs

As with **-ir** verbs, watch the difference between the first/second-person singular endings and the third-person singular (see Day 1, Section I). For example: **je vends, tu vends, il vend**; **je bats, tu bats, il bat**.

Students sometimes write the third-person plural form with an intrusive **r** before the ending, e.g. **ils se battrent** instead of **ils se battent** [they are fighting]. This probably arises from confusion with the stem of the future/conditional which is found by taking the infinitive and removing the final **-e**, giving e.g. **ils se battront** [they will fight]. Note that the stem of the present tense is found by removing the final **-re** from the infinitive, giving **ils se battent**.

Complete the sentences below with the correct form of the present tense.

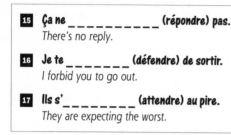

15 Ça ne _ _ _ _ _ _ _ _ _ _ (répondre) pas.
There's no reply.

16 Je te _ _ _ _ _ _ _ _ (défendre) de sortir.
I forbid you to go out.

17 Ils s'_ _ _ _ _ _ _ _ _ (attendre) au pire.
They are expecting the worst.

V Irregular verbs

Irregular verbs are often also very common verbs, so it is extremely important to learn them thoroughly, for example: **avoir, aller, connaître, croire, devoir, dire, être, faire, mourir, naître, ouvrir, pouvoir, prendre, recevoir, savoir, venir, voir, vouloir**, etc. Check in a reference grammar if you are unsure of any of these.

It is also important to remember that compounds of irregular verbs usually follow the same pattern of conjugation as the basic verb, e.g. **satisfaire** is conjugated like **faire**, and **devenir** like **venir**, hence **ils satisfont** is like **ils font**, and **ils deviennent** is like **ils viennent**.

It helps to learn irregular verbs in families, for example: verbs ending in **-evoir**, like **apercevoir, percevoir** and **recevoir**, and verbs ending in **-ndre**, like **craindre** and **joindre**.

Complete the sentences below with the correct form of the present tense.

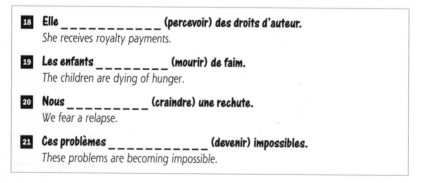

18 Elle _ _ _ _ _ _ _ _ _ _ _ _ (percevoir) des droits d'auteur.
She receives royalty payments.

19 Les enfants _ _ _ _ _ _ _ _ (mourir) de faim.
The children are dying of hunger.

20 Nous _ _ _ _ _ _ _ _ _ (craindre) une rechute.
We fear a relapse.

21 Ces problèmes _ _ _ _ _ _ _ _ _ _ _ (devenir) impossibles.
These problems are becoming impossible.

Correct the errors in the following sentences written by students.

> **22** **Les films hollywoodiens ne nous satisfaisent plus.**
> Hollywood films no longer satisfy us.
>
> **23** **Ils apprendent leur métier.**
> They are learning their trade.
>
> **24** **Ils ne recevent pas assez d'argent.**
> They do not receive enough money.

VI Function

The English progressive, e.g. 'I am reading the paper' is normally expressed by a simple present tense in French, **je lis le journal**. If it is really important to stress the ongoing nature of the activity, you should use **être en train de** + infinitive. For example:

> **Ils sont en train de se réorganiser.**
> [They are busy reorganizing themselves.]

The use of **être** + present participle is not permissible, tempting though it may be to an Anglophone!

Rewrite the following sentences in order to stress the ongoing nature of the activity concerned.

> **25** **Ils rénovent l'appartement.**
> They are refurbishing the flat.
>
> **26** **Nous refaisons tout son travail.**
> We are redoing all his work.

VII Final note

It is very important to be sure of the formation of the present tense, not only because you will use it very frequently, but also because the first-person plural (**nous**) form gives you the stem for the imperfect indicative, and the third-person plural form gives you the stem for the present subjunctive. **Nous choisiss-ons**, for example, gives the stem for the imperfect indicative, **je choisiss-ais**, while **ils choisiss-ent** gives the stem for the present subjunctive, **je choisiss-e**.

Give the first-person singular imperfect indicative and present subjunctive forms of the following verbs:

> **27** – **28** **recevoir**
>
> **29** – **30** **prendre**

See for further information
Hawkins and Towell, Chapter 7
Jubb and Rouxeville, Chapter 1
Judge and Healey, Chapter 10, §3.2.1
Byrne and Churchill, §§345–78
Ferrar, §§3, 8–12

It is essential to know how to present and discuss statistics and numbers in French. Vocabulary is often the key to success, and today's exercises will help to increase your competence and confidence in this area.

I Number
There are several words in French, each with a particular range of meanings, to translate the word 'number' itself and the related notion of 'figure(s)'. Study the following examples to refresh your memory.

NOMBRE number (concept); quantity
un nombre entier a whole number
un nombre positif/négatif a positive/negative number
bon nombre de gens a good many people
le nombre des chômeurs the number of unemployed

NUMÉRO – numbered item (often in a series)
un numéro de téléphone telephone number
le numéro 7 the number 7

le numéro un de l'opposition the leader of the opposition
un vieux numéro a back number or issue (of newspaper or journal)

CHIFFRE figure, digit; statistic(s); total number
un numéro à cinq chiffres a five-figure or -digit number
les chiffres du mois sont bons this month's figures are good
les chiffres officiels du chômage the official unemployment figures
Note also **le chiffre d'affaires** turnover

Fill in the gaps in the sentences below with an appropriate French translation for 'number' or 'figure(s)'.

---

1   C'est le _ _ _ _ _ _ _ _ _ _ _ un mondial du squash.
He's the world's number one squash player.

2 - **3**   Donnez-moi un _ _ _ _ _ _ _ _ _ _ _ _ à trois _ _ _ _ _ _ _ _ _ _ _.
Give me a three-figure number.

4   Un grand _ _ _ _ _ _ _ _ _ _ d'étudiants faisaient la queue devant le réfectoire.
A large number of students were queuing outside the refectory.

5 Les _ _ _ _ _ _ _ _ _ officiels montrent une nette amélioration du taux du chômage.

Official figures show a clear improvement in the unemployment rate.

6 Je cherche un vieux _ _ _ _ _ _ _ _ _ _ _ _ _ _ de Positif.

I'm looking for a back number of Positif.

7 On ne sait pas encore le _ _ _ _ _ _ _ _ _ _ _ de morts.

They don't yet know the number of dead.

II Useful verbs

atteindre to reach
compter to number, to have, e.g. **La France compte deux millions de chômeurs**. France has two million unemployed.

On compte deux millions de chômeurs. There is a total of two million unemployed.
s'élever à to amount/come to, to stand at
passer de ... à to go from ... to

Complete the following sentences with appropriate expressions from the list above.

8 Le taux de chômage a _ _ _ _ _ _ _ _ _ _ _ _ _ un niveau sans précédent.

The unemployment rate has reached an unprecedented level.

9 Le nombre des victimes _ _ _ _ _ _ _ _ _ à 18.

The casualty figures stand at 18.

10 On _ _ _ _ _ _ _ _ _ 450 cas de fièvre aphteuse.

There is a total of 450 cases of foot and mouth disease.

11 Le prix d'achat est _ _ _ _ _ _ _ _ _ _ _ _ _ _ de 25 à 30 francs.

The price has gone up from 25 to 30 francs.

With the following verbs, note which are intransitive (cannot take a direct object), and which can be either transitive (can take a direct object) or intransitive.

s'accroître to grow, increase (intransitive)
augmenter to grow, rise (intransitive); increase (transitive and intransitive)
se développer to grow (intransitive)

progresser de to increase, rise (by) (intransitive)
baisser to go down (intransitive); to lower (transitive)
diminuer to decrease (intransitive); to reduce, cut (transitive)

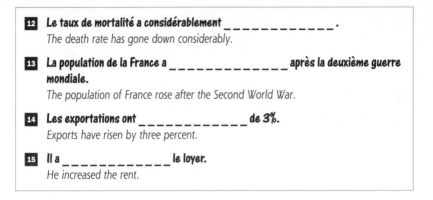

12 **Le taux de mortalité a considérablement** _ _ _ _ _ _ _ _ _ _ _ _ **.**
The death rate has gone down considerably.

13 **La population de la France a** _ _ _ _ _ _ _ _ _ _ _ _ _ **après la deuxième guerre mondiale.**
The population of France rose after the Second World War.

14 **Les exportations ont** _ _ _ _ _ _ _ _ _ _ _ _ **de 3%.**
Exports have risen by three percent.

15 **Il a** _ _ _ _ _ _ _ _ _ _ _ _ **le loyer.**
He increased the rent.

III Useful nouns, adjectives, prepositions and other expressions

l'accroissement increase
l'augmentation increase
la progression increase
être en progression to be increasing
la hausse rise
être en hausse to be rising
la baisse fall
être en baisse to be falling, coming down
la chute fall, drop
la diminution decrease, reduction
le niveau level
le taux de the rate of
supérieur/inférieur à higher/lower than
contre as compared to

sur out of, e.g. **quatre sur dix** four out of ten
en moyenne on average
dont including, e.g. **3,1 millions de chômeurs, dont 1,1 million depuis au moins un an**
3.1 million unemployed, including 1.1 million who have been unemployed for at least a year.
soit i.e. (that is), e.g. **1 321 000 femmes travaillent à temps partiel, soit 15,5% de la population active féminine.**
1,321,000 women are in part-time employment, i.e. 15.5% of the total number of women in work.

Complete the following sentences with appropriate expressions from the list above.

16 **25% des femmes entre vingt et soixante-quatre ans vivent seules,** _ _ _ _ _ **600 000 avec un enfant à charge.**
25% of women between the ages of 20 and 64 live alone, including 600,000 who are supporting a child.

17 – 18 **Les femmes perçoivent** _ _ _ _ _ _ _ _ _ _ **des salaires** _ _ _ _ _ _ _ _ _ _ **à ceux des hommes.**
Women's pay on average is lower than men's.

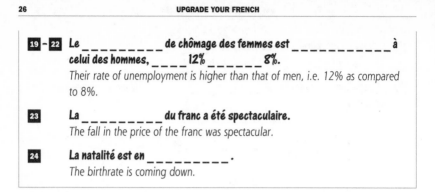

19 - 22 Le _ _ _ _ _ _ _ _ _ de chômage des femmes est _ _ _ _ _ _ _ _ _ _ _ à
celui des hommes, _ _ _ _ 12% _ _ _ _ _ _ 8%.
*Their rate of unemployment is higher than that of men, i.e. 12% as compared
to 8%.*

23 La _ _ _ _ _ _ _ _ _ du franc a été spectaculaire.
The fall in the price of the franc was spectacular.

24 La natalité est en _ _ _ _ _ _ _ _ _ _ .
The birthrate is coming down.

IV   Presentation of numbers

French usage of commas and full stops to indicate decimals and multiples is
markedly different from English usage. Careful attention to this will give your French
greater authenticity.

- Where English uses a full stop to separate whole numbers from decimals, e.g.
  5.7, French uses a comma, e.g. 5,7.
- Where English uses a comma in a multiple such as 1,300,000, to separate
  hundreds from thousands, and thousands from millions, French normally leaves
  a typographical space, e.g. 1 300 000.

Correct the errors in the following sentences.

25 Le nombre des femmes qui exercent un emploi a augmenté de 1,750,000.
The number of women in work has gone up by 1,750,000.

26 Cela équivaut à 15.5% de la population active féminine.
That is the equivalent of 15.5% of working women.

Writing out numbers in words can also be a problem. If you are unsure when to put
an **-s** on the end of **cent** and **quatre-vingt**, check in a reference grammar.
Mistakes with thousands and millions are particularly common, but are easily
corrected if you remember the following:

- **mille** (thousand) never takes a plural **-s**. Nor is it ever preceded by an indefinite article.
- If you want to speak about an unspecified number of thousands, use **des
  milliers** + **de** + noun.
- **million** [million] and **milliard** [billion] both behave as expressions of quantity
  (see Day 8), i.e. they take **de** before a noun. Note that they also take a plural
  -s, e.g. **un million de chômeurs** a million unemployed; **trois millions de
  francs** three million francs; **dix milliards de francs** ten billion francs

Rewrite the following, giving the numbers in words.

27 **Il a gagné 1 000 livres.**
He has won a thousand pounds.

28 **L'an 2000.**
The year 2000.

29 **Ils ont perdu 2 000 000 francs.**
They lost 2,000,000 francs.

Finally, complete the following sentence.

30 **Il y en avait _ _ _ _ _ _ _ _ _ _ _ .**
There were thousands of them.

See for further information
Hawkins and Towell, 6.1–6.9.1
Judge and Healey, Chapter 2, §§5.1–5.5
Ferrar, §§134–40

Do you lose marks for forgetting to make adjectives agree? A lot of students do. Do you find it difficult to spot where you have gone wrong until someone else points it out to you? The following exercises are intended to help you improve your ability to check and correct your own work.

I Agreements for gender

Adjectives must agree in gender (masculine or feminine) with the noun/pronoun which they qualify. First, you must know the gender of the noun. If in doubt, check, and don't assume that a noun which ends in **-e** is feminine. Students often make mistakes with **un groupe**, **un manque**, **un problème**, **un système**. Also note that nouns ending in **-ment** are all masculine (with only one exception, **la jument** mare), and nouns ending in **-tion** are feminine.

The feminine of an adjective is normally formed by adding an **-e** to the end of the masculine form, e.g. **français** (m); **française** (f). Some adjectives double their final consonant as well as adding an **-e** in the feminine, e.g. **naturel, naturelle**; **européen, européenne**; **gros, grosse**; **net, nette**. There are also some other special forms to be remembered. The following are often forgotten:

- Adjectives ending in **-c** form their feminine in **-che**, e.g. **blanc, blanche**. Exceptions include **public, publique**; **grec, grecque**.
- Adjectives ending in **-er** form their feminine in **-ère**, e.g. **premier, première**.
- Adjectives ending in **-f** form their feminine in **-ve**, e.g. **vif, vive.**

Make the adjectives in the following agree as necessary. The masculine singular form is given in brackets.

---

1 **Que pensez-vous de l'Union (européen)?**
What do you think of the European Union?

2 **Il a une démarche très (léger).**
He walks with a very light step.

3 **Elle mène une vie très (actif).**
She leads a very busy life.

4 **J'adore la cuisine (grec).**
I love Greek food.

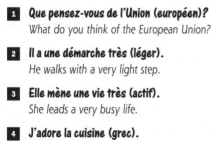

Remember that adjectives whose masculine form ends in a silent **-e** do not change in the feminine, e.g. **la vie facile**, but adjectives and past participles which end in **-é** add a further **-e** in the feminine, e.g. **une porte fermée**.

Five adjectives – **beau**, **fou**, **mou**, **nouveau**, **vieux** – have a special form used before a masculine singular word beginning with a vowel or mute **h**: **bel**, **fol**, **mol**, **nouvel**, **vieil**.

Make the adjectives in the following agree as necessary. The masculine singular form is given in brackets.

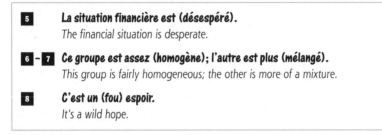

> **5**   **La situation financière est (désespéré).**
>   *The financial situation is desperate.*
>
> **6** - **7**   **Ce groupe est assez (homogène); l'autre est plus (mélangé).**
>   *This group is fairly homogeneous; the other is more of a mixture.*
>
> **8**   **C'est un (fou) espoir.**
>   *It's a wild hope.*

II Agreements for number

Adjectives must agree in number (singular/plural) as well as in gender with the noun/pronoun which they qualify. In most cases, the plural of an adjective is formed by adding an **-s** to the singular form. There are some exceptions to note:

- Adjectives which end in **-s** or **-x** do not change in the masculine plural form, e.g. **des costumes gris, des gens heureux**.
- Adjectives which end in **-al**, with only a few exceptions, e.g. **banal**, **banals**, form their masculine plural in **-aux**, e.g. **les champions nationaux**, but note that the feminine plural is regular, e.g. **les routes nationales**.
- Confusion often arises between the masculine and feminine plural forms of adjectives in **-al**, and **-el**:

  Masculine plural: **des concours nationaux**   **des résultats exceptionnels**
  Feminine plural: **les routes nationales**   **des subventions**
                                                 exceptionnelles

- Adjectives which end in **-eau** form their masculine plural in **-eaux**, e.g. **les nouveaux voisins**.
- The masculine plural of **tout** is the irregular, **TOUS**. The feminine plural, **toutes**, is regular.

Make the adjectives in the following agree as necessary.

9   *Ce sont des fleurs (artificiel).*
They are artificial flowers.

10   *Fais de (beau) rêves!*
Sweet dreams!

11 – 12   *(Tout) les (divers) catégories ont été étudiées.*
All the various categories have been examined.

13 – 14   *On a convoqué une réunion de (tout) les directeurs (régional).*
A meeting of all the regional directors has been convened.

15   *La consommation des huiles (végétal) a diminué de moitié.*
Consumption of vegetable oils has gone down by a half.

It is reasonably easy to remember to make adjectives agree when they stand next to the noun which they qualify, but be careful not to overlook agreements when the adjective is connected to a noun/pronoun by a linking verb, such as **être**, **devenir**, **paraître**. For example:

> **Les fenêtres sont fermées.**
> [The windows are shut.]
> **Ses cousins sont devenus riches.**
> [His cousins became rich.]
> **Elle paraît épuisée.**
> [She looks worn out.]

Be particularly careful in a relative clause; always check back to find the subject. For example:

> **Elle a trouvé deux annonces qui sont vraiment prometteuses.**
> [She has found two adverts which are really promising.]

Make the adjectives in the following agree as necessary:

16   *Les Etats-Unis semblent (capable) de tout faire.*
The United States seem capable of doing anything.

17   *Tous ceux qui étaient (absent) ont perdu leur place.*
All those who were absent have lost their place.

Now practise your checking strategy. Read the following passage, imagining you wrote it in an examination and are now checking it through. Look at each adjective and check if it agrees as it should. Correct it if necessary.

---

18 – 23   Modèles féminin des années cinquante

A l'aube des années soixante, la société française connaît des changements social, politiques et économiques liés à l'élargissement des classes moyen d'une part, et à l'incertitude de l'époque d'autre part. Au sortir de la guerre, les équilibres mondial paraissent en effet bien fragile, et ce d'autant plus que les conflits politiques sont multiple; guerre de Corée, guerre d'Indochine, guerre d'Algérie.

(Extrait de: V. Aebischer et Sonia Dayan-Herzbrun, 'Cinéma et destins de femmes', in *Cahiers Internationaux de Sociologie*, LXXX (Paris, Presses Universitaires de France, 1986), p. 149)

How many corrections have you made? If you found six, go on to the next exercise. If you found fewer (or more!) than six, try again.

III   Common problems with agreements

- If an adjective qualifies two or more nouns of different genders, e.g. **un frère et une sœur inséparables** [an inseparable brother and sister], the adjective is masculine plural.
- When a noun is acompanied by an adjective and also by a phrase (**de** + noun), be careful to make the adjective agree with the noun which it qualifies, and not necessarily with the noun nearest to it. For example:

du point de vue médical
[from the medical point of view] (masculine agreement with **point**)

- With expressions of the type, **c'est l'un des monuments les plus célèbres du monde** [it's one of the most famous monuments in the world], the adjective describes all the monuments and so is plural.
- After **quelque chose, rien, quoi**, use **de** + masculine adjective. For example:

quelque chose de bon
[something good]

- Remember always to make adjectives agree with the noun which they qualify, even when the adjectives appear at the beginning of the sentence/clause and the noun follows. For example:

Superbe et arrogante, elle détourna la tête.
[Haughtily and arrogantly, she looked away.]

Correct the errors of agreement in the following sentences.

24 *C'est l'un des plus beau châteaux de France.*
It's one of the finest châteaux in France.

25 *Elle souffre de maux de tête continuel.*
She suffers from persistent headaches.

26 *Seul, elle ne réussira jamais à s'en sortir.*
On her own, she will never manage to cope.

27 *Est-ce que vous y avez trouvé quelque chose d'intéressante?*
Did you find something interesting in it?

Sometimes students make agreements which should NOT be made:

- Numbers, with the exception of the nouns **million**, **billion**, do NOT usually take a plural **-s**, thus: **à l'aube des années soixante** [in the early 1960s] in the text above.
- Adverbs such as **beaucoup, ensemble** are invariable. For example:

Ils travaillent ensemble.
[They are working together.]

Correct the error of agreement in the following.

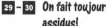 **28** *La mère et son fils sont restés ensembles.*
The mother and her son stayed together.

Particular care is needed with **même**. Used as an adjective, it agrees with the noun which it accompanies, but used as an adverb (meaning 'even'), it is invariable. For example:

> **On trouve toujours les mêmes fautes!**
> [You always find the same (adjective) mistakes!]
> **Même certains adultes s'intéressent aux livres pour enfants.**
> [Even (adverb) some adults are interested in children's books.]

Agreement is necessary in one of the following cases. Which one?

29 - **30** *On fait toujours les (même) exercices. C'est à dégoûter (même) les plus assidus!*
We're always doing the same exercises. It's enough to put off even the most diligent!

See for further information
Hawkins and Towell, 4.7–4.11.4
Jubb and Rouxeville, Chapter 15
Judge and Healey, Chapter 11
Byrne and Churchill, §§127–38
Ferrar, §§109–13
See also Day 13 for past participle agreements.

Upgrade your style: Alternatives to adverbs

*Your French will often sound more natural if you can find an alternative to an adverb ending in **-ment**. Particularly to be avoided are very cumbersome, lengthy adverbs.*

I Adverbial phrases
A useful alternative is an adverbial phrase introduced by a preposition. Most productive of all are the prepositions **avec** and **sans**.

avec attention attentively	**sans distinction** indiscriminately
avec circonspection cautiously, guardedly	**sans intelligence** unintelligently
	sans interruption uninterruptedly
avec un peu de chance hopefully	**sans ménagement** bluntly
avec intelligence intelligently	(of speech); roughly,
avec patience patiently	unceremoniously
avec reconnaissance thankfully	It is also possible to use **sans** +
avec soin carefully	infinitive, e.g. **sans hésiter**
sans cérémonie unceremoniously	unhesitatingly
sans cesse continuously	**sans pouvoir rien faire** helplessly

Complete the following, in each case using an adverbial phrase introduced by **avec** or **sans** to translate the English adverb.

1 Elle a balayé nos objections _.
She swept our objections roughly aside.

2 Ils ont avancé _ _ _ _ _ _ _ _ _ _ _ _ _ _ _ _ _ _ _.
They moved cautiously forward.

3 Nous avons regardé l'avalanche _ _ _ _ _ _ _ _ _ _ _ _ _ _ _ _ _ _ _.
We watched the avalanche helplessly.

4 On a massacré les animaux _ _ _ _ _ _ _ _ _ _ _ _ _ _ _ _ _ _.
The animals were indiscriminately slaughtered.

5 _ _ _ _ _ _ _ _ _ _ _ _ _ _ _ _ _ _, nous y arriverons avant la tombée de la nuit.
Hopefully, we will get there before nightfall.

It is possible to form other adverbial phrases introduced by **d'un air**, **d'une façon/manière**, **de façon/manière**, **d'un ton/sur un ton**, and **par**.

d'un air fâché angrily	**d'un ton morne** dully
d'une façon/manière triste sadly	**d'un ton sec** drily
d'une façon/manière désastreuse disastrously	**sur un ton solennel** solemnly
de façon inattendue unexpectedly	**par hasard** accidentally
d'un ton bourru gruffly	**par manque de générosité** ungenerously

Complete the following sentences with appropriate expressions from the list above.

6 Je l'ai découvert _ _ _ _ _ _ _ _ _ _ _ _ _ _ _ _.
   I came across it accidentally.

7 Elle a annoncé la nouvelle _ _ _ _ _ _ _ _ _ _ _ _ _ _ _ _ _.
   She announced the news very solemnly.

8 Surtout ne te fatigue pas trop! fit-elle _ _ _ _ _ _ _ _ _ _ _ _.
   Don't kill yourself! she said drily.

9 Ils ont échoué _ _ _ _ _ _ _ _ _ _ _ _ _ _ _ _.
   They failed disastrously.

10 _ _ _ _ _ _ _ _ _ _ _ _ _ _, il a quitté la table et est parti.
   Unexpectedly, he got up from the table and left.

II   Adjectives as adverbs

Some adjectives can be used as adverbs in certain set expressions with particular verbs. When used in this way, these adjectives always remain in the masculine singular.

parler bas to talk quietly	**deviner/viser juste** to guess/aim correctly
voir clair to see clearly	
parler fort to talk loudly	**peser lourd** to weigh heavily

Complete the following sentences.

11 Avec ses lunettes, elle y voit _ _ _ _ _ _ _ _ _.
   With her glasses, she can see properly.

12 Vous avez deviné _ _ _ _ _ _ _ _.
   You have guessed correctly.

13 Ils parlent trop _ _ _ _ _ _ pour que je les entende.
   They talking too quietly for me to hear them.

III Some idiomatic phrases

First, a reminder of some adverbial phrases that you should already know, but which you perhaps don't use as often as you could to translate English adverbs.

à peu près almost, nearly; about	**en particulier** particularly
au juste exactly	**par la suite** subsequently
avant tout essentially	**peu à peu** gradually
d'habitude usually	**tout à coup**; **tout d'un coup**
de plus en plus increasingly	suddenly
en général generally	**tout à fait** completely
en gros roughly, broadly	**tout de suite** immediately

Complete the following sentences with appropriate expressions from the list above.

14 C'est _ _ _ _ _ _ _ _ _ _ _ _ _ _ _ terminé.
It's almost finished.

15 _ _ _ _ _ _ _ _ _ _ _ _ on l'a transféré au bureau de Paris.
Subsequently he was transferred to the Paris office.

16 Il a beaucoup plu, dans l'ouest _ .
It has rained a lot, particularly in the west.

17 Ce qu'il recherche _ _ _ _ _ _ _ _ _ _ _ _ _ _ _ c'est la tranquillité.
What he wants essentially is peace and quiet.

18 Qu'est-ce que vous recherchez _ _ _ _ _ _ _ _ _ _ _ _ ?
What are you looking for exactly?

Next, some adverbial phrases which you could usefully add to your active vocabulary if you don't already know them:

à bon compte cheaply, easily	**à tue-tête** very loudly, at the top of
s'en tirer à bon compte to get off	one's voice
lightly	**de bon gré** willingly
à bon escient advisedly	**de mauvais gré** reluctantly
à brûle-pourpoint abruptly,	**du bout des lèvres** half-heartedly
point-blank	(e.g. of laughter, response)
à contrecœur reluctantly	**en définitive** finally
à dessein deliberately, intentionally	**en flèche** steeply (rise, e.g. of prices,
à juste titre quite rightly	inflation)
à la légère lightly	**en mon/son** (as appropriate) **for**
à ma/sa (as appropriate) **grande**	**intérieur** privately, secretly (in
surprise surprisingly	one's heart)
à pic steeply (rise, fall)	**petit à petit** gradually
à tort wrongly	**sur-le-champ** immediately

Complete the following sentences using appropriate expressions from the list.

---

19 **Les prix sont montés** _ _ _ _ _ _ _ _ _ _ .
Prices have risen steeply.

20 **Elle espère** _ _ _ _ _ _ _ _ _ _ _ _ _ _ _ _ **qu'ils partiront bientôt.**
She secretly hopes that they will soon leave.

21 **Ils s'en sont tirés** _ _ _ _ _ _ _ _ _ _ _ _ _ _ _ _ _ _ .
They got off lightly.

22 **Les étudiants ont ri** _ _ _ _ _ _ _ _ _ _ _ _ _ .
The students laughed half-heartedly.

23 **Elle lui a prêté la voiture** _ _ _ _ _ _ _ _ _ _ _ _ _ _ .
She reluctantly lent him the car.

24 _ , **elle a réussi son permis de conduire.**
Surprisingly, she passed her driving test.

25 **Elle lui a demandé** _ _ _ _ _ _ _ _ _ _ _ _ _ _ _ _ _ **combien il gagnait par mois.**
She asked him abruptly how much he earned a month.

IV Impersonal expressions

These expressions are well known, but are often overlooked as an alternative to adverbs.

---

il est clair que clearly   **il est possible que** (+ subjunctive)
il est évident que obviously   possibly

Complete the following sentences using appropriate impersonal expressions.

---

26 _ **qu'il n'en sait rien.**
Obviously he knows nothing about it.

27 _ _ _ _ _ _ _ _ _ _ _ _ _ _ **qu'ils arrivent plus tard.**
They may possibly arrive later.

V Transpositions

Instead of using an adverb ending in **-ment** to qualify an adjective or participle, you could try using an adjectival phrase formed from **de** (+ indefinite article) + noun + adjective. For example:

> **d'une lenteur exaspérante**
> [infuriatingly slow]
> **de conception individualisée**
> [individually designed]

Following the same principle of using a noun + adjective instead of an adjective qualified by an adverb, note the expression: **avoir la conviction intime que** [to be quietly confident that]. Elsewhere, it may sometimes be possible to use a noun, or a noun and adjective instead of a verb qualified by an adverb. For example:

La France est sa vraie patrie.
[France is where he truly belongs.]

Complete the following sentences using appropriate transpositions.

28 **Ses toiles sont d'** _ .
His pictures are amazingly varied.

29 **Elle a la** _ **qu'il sera reçu.**
She is quietly confident that he will pass.

30 **Le sport est l'** _ _ _ _ _ _ _ **de sa vie.**
Sport is what he really loves.

See for further information
Hawkins and Towell, Chapter 5
Ferrar, §§114–16

I   Some basic problems

You may find that you lose marks unnecessarily for overlooking some of the following basic points when you are under pressure. Bear these in mind when checking through your work:

- Always check the gender of your nouns and the gender of the accompanying articles.
- Remember that the preposition **à** combines with the definite articles **le/les** to give **au/aux**, and that the preposition **de** combines with them to give **du/des**.
- Watch out for singular nouns and adjectives beginning with a vowel or inaspirate **h** and remember to use **l'** before them, and not **le/la**, e.g. **l'Ancien Régime, l'université, l'hôtel, l'heure**. Also remember to use **de l'** and not **du, de la**, e.g. **de l'humour, de l'aide**, and to reduce **de** to **d'**, e.g. **une bouteille d'huile**.
- Try to learn which nouns and adjectives begin with an aspirate **h** and do not reduce the article before them to **l'** or **de l'**, e.g. **le hareng, le hasard, le héros, le Haut Moyen Age, le fait du hasard, de la haine**.
- Also remember not to reduce **de** to **d'**, e.g. **de haute importance**.

Fill in the gaps in the following sentences as appropriate.

---

1 Il faut mettre _ _ _ _ huile dans les rouages.
You must oil the works.

2 _ _ _ hiérarchie est tout à fait inaltérable.
The hierarchy is quite immutable.

3 C'est un produit _ _ _ _ haute qualité.
This is a high-quality product.

Read the following sentences and correct any errors which you find.

---

4 Notre pays appartient à la groupe des Sept.
Our country is a member of the group of Seven.

5 La authenticité des documents est mise en doute.
The authenticity of the documents is called into question.

---

6 **Je n'ai pas la habitude de les voir le weekend.**
I don't usually see them at the weekend.

7 **Le hasard a voulu que je trouve la source de les citations.**
Chance would have it that I found the source of the quotations.

8 **C'est la unique voie qui y mène.**
It's the only way to get there.

You should have found five errors – one in each sentence. If you didn't find as many, or found more, try again!

II   Mistaken omission of article

Perhaps the most common mistake which students make is missing out articles in contexts where they would not be used in English.

First, the well-known generalizing definite article, as used for example after verbs of liking and disliking. For example:

> **Nous aimons le chocolat.**
> [We love chocolate.]
> **Il déteste la choucroute.**
> [He hates sauerkraut.]

The generalizing definite article is also used with abstract nouns used in a general sense. For example:

> **La perfection n'est pas de ce monde.**
> [Perfection does not belong to this world.]
> **Le stress est dangereux pour la santé.**
> [Stress is a danger to health.]

Do you always remember to use a generalizing definite article when necessary after **de**? For example:

> **le monde *des* idées**
> [the world of ideas]
> **les racines *du* colonialisme**
> [the roots of colonialism]
> **l'évolution *de la* science**
> [the advancement of science]

Be careful to distinguish examples like those above from the very common French pattern of noun + **de** + noun where **de** + noun (with no article before the noun) acts as an adjective qualifying the first noun. For example:

> **une femme de chambre**
> [a chambermaid]

une lampe de chevet
[a bedside lamp]
un rendez-vous d'affaires
[a business appointment]

Contrast the latter example with **le français des affaires** [business French], where 'business' means business in general.

Complete the sentences below by choosing between the alternatives in brackets.

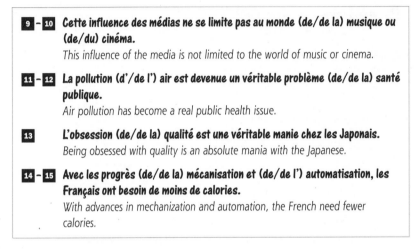

9 – 10 Cette influence des médias ne se limite pas au monde (de/de la) musique ou (de/du) cinéma.
This influence of the media is not limited to the world of music or cinema.

11 – 12 La pollution (d'/de l') air est devenue un véritable problème (de/de la) santé publique.
Air pollution has become a real public health issue.

13 L'obsession (de/de la) qualité est une véritable manie chez les Japonais.
Being obsessed with quality is an absolute mania with the Japanese.

14 – 15 Avec les progrès (de/de la) mécanisation et (de/de l') automatisation, les Français ont besoin de moins de calories.
With advances in mechanization and automation, the French need fewer calories.

A second problem is the plural indefinite article, **des.** It often has no equivalent in English. For example:

Des centaines de jeunes sont morts.
[Hundreds of young people have died.]
Ce sont des amateurs.
[They are amateurs.]

If in doubt, a good rule of thumb is to try the sentence in the singular. If you would use **un/une** in the singular, then make sure you use **des** in the plural. Thus, with the examples above, an indefinite article would have been used in the singular. For example:

Une centaine de jeunes sont morts.
[About a hundred young people have died.]
C'est un amateur.
[He is an amateur.]

Be careful if there is a plural adjective before the noun, because **des** will change to **de/d'**. For example:

De telles situations me font peur.
[Such situations frighten me.]
Est-ce qu'il y a d'autres cours qui vous intéressent?
[Are there any other classes which interest you?]

Rewrite the following sentences, putting the underlined words into the plural.

---

16   *Je pourrais vous en donner <u>une dizaine</u> d'exemples.*
I could give you a dozen examples. (I could give you dozens of examples.)

17   *Je n'ai jamais eu <u>un tel problème</u>.*
I've never had such a problem. (I've never had such problems.)

18   *C'est <u>un fanatique</u>.*
He is a fanatic. (They are fanatics.)

III   Choosing between *des* and *les*

Often the best way to decide between the plural indefinite article, **des**, and the plural definite article, **les**, is to try the sentence in the singular. For example:

Les phoques sont des mammifères.
[Seals are mammals.]
Le phoque est un mammifère.
[The seal is a mammal.]
Ces hommes sont les représentants de la communauté.
[These men are the representatives of the community.]
Cet homme est le représentant de la commmunauté.
[This man is the representative of the community.]

Complete the sentences below by filling the gaps with **des** or **les** as appropriate.

---

19   *La dépression peut aussi causer _ _ _ problèmes physiques.*
Depression can also cause physical problems.

20   *Ces étudiants sont _ _ _ Ecossais.*
These students are Scots.

21   *Cela va provoquer _ _ _ réactions.*
People are bound to react.

IV   Choosing between *des* and *de/d'*

A shorthand formula to remember is the following:

de + les gives **des**, but
de + des gives **de/d'**

In other words, the definite article, **les,** combines with **de** to give **des**. For example:

> **les résultats des élections**
> [the results of the elections]

But the plural indefinite article **des** is omitted after **de**. For example:

> **il a besoin de livres**
> [he needs (some) books]

Complete the following sentences by filling the gaps with **des** or **de/d'** as appropriate.

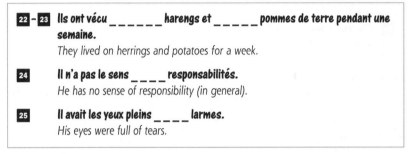

> **22 – 23** **Ils ont vécu _ _ _ _ _ _ harengs et _ _ _ _ _ pommes de terre pendant une semaine.**
> *They lived on herrings and potatoes for a week.*

> **24** **Il n'a pas le sens _ _ _ _ responsabilités.**
> *He has no sense of responsibility (in general).*

> **25** **Il avait les yeux pleins _ _ _ _ larmes.**
> *His eyes were full of tears.*

Watch out for the following:

- Before a plural adjective, the plural indefinite article, **des**, changes to **de/d'** (see Section II above), e.g. **de telles idées** [such ideas]. But this does not apply when the adjective and noun refer to something which is seen as a single unit. For example:

des jeunes hommes
[young men]
des petits pains
[bread rolls]
des grands magasins
[department stores]

- With the direct object of a negative verb, **de** is normally substituted for **des** and also for **un(e)**, **du**, **de la**, **de l'**. For example:

Je n'y vois pas d'inconvénients.
[I can't see any drawbacks in it.]
Nous n'avons pas de voiture.
[We don't have a car.]
Je n'ai pas de thé.
[I don't have any tea.]

Correct the following sentences by choosing between the alternatives in brackets.

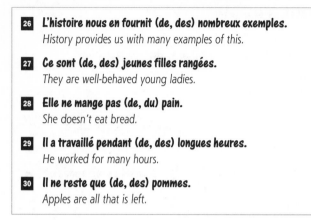

26 **L'histoire nous en fournit (de, des) nombreux exemples.**
History provides us with many examples of this.

27 **Ce sont (de, des) jeunes filles rangées.**
They are well-behaved young ladies.

28 **Elle ne mange pas (de, du) pain.**
She doesn't eat bread.

29 **Il a travaillé pendant (de, des) longues heures.**
He worked for many hours.

30 **Il ne reste que (de, des) pommes.**
Apples are all that is left.

Did you hesitate because of **ne . . . que** in sentence 30? In fact, **ne . . . que** is not negative in meaning, and so the rule given above does not apply. See Day 18 for further practice.

See for further information
Hawkins and Towell, 2.1–2.6.8
Jubb and Rouxeville, Chapter 14
Judge and Healey, Chapter 2, §1
Byrne and Churchill, §§24–46
Ferrar, §§70–87

Upgrade your vocabulary: Quantifiers

*You can make an immediate improvement to your work if you make a conscious effort to find alternatives for the overused **beaucoup** [a lot], **la plupart** [most of] and **quelques** [some]. Today's exercises encourage you to make active use of a range of different expressions. Remember that variety of expression is as important as accuracy if you want to do yourself full justice in exams.*

I Ring the changes on *beaucoup*

bien + du/de la/des a lot of, e.g. **elle s'est donné bien du mal** she has gone to a lot of trouble
bien des gens a lot of people
énormément (de) a tremendous number/amount of
bon nombre de a good many
un certain nombre de a number of, a good many; some
un grand nombre de many
un très grand nombre de a great many, very many
nombre de a number of
être nombreux, e.g. **ils étaient nombreux** there were a great many of them

de nombreux + noun, e.g. **de nombreux exemples** many, numerous examples (Note the use of **de** instead of **des**, because the adjective **nombreux** precedes the noun – see Day 7, Section IV.)
pas mal de (informal French), e.g. **j'ai pas mal de travail** I've got quite a lot of work
(une) quantité de/des quantités de (informal French) a lot of
Note that it is not permissible to say *****très beaucoup**!

Fill in the gaps in the following sentences by using an appropriate expression from the list above.

---

1 _____ d'étudiants ont assisté à la conférence.
A good many students attended the lecture.

2 Il a passé de _____ années en France.
He has spent many years in France.

3 On a trouvé _____ de témoins.
A number of witnesses were found.

4 Il a fumé _ _ _ _ _ _ _ _ _ _ _ _ _ _ _ _ _ de cigares.
He smoked a tremendous number of cigars.

5 Nous étions _ _ _ _ _ _ _ _ _ _ _ _ _ _ à ne pas le reconnaître.
There were a lot of us who did not recognize him.

6 _ d'étudiants ont des dettes.
Very many students are in debt.

7 C'était il y a _ _ _ _ _ _ _ _ des années.
That was a good many years ago.

8 Vous avez _ _ _ _ _ _ _ _ _ _ _ _ d'amis. (informal French)
You've got quite a lot of friends.

9 Il y avait une _ _ _ _ _ _ _ _ _ _ _ _ _ _ _ _ de touristes incroyable. (informal French)
There were an incredible number of tourists.

If you want to translate 'not many', 'not much', the best solution, rather than **pas beaucoup**, is often **peu**. For example:

> **Il y a peu d'espoir.**
> [There's not much hope.]

Note also that you can use **peu** with an adjective, instead of **pas très** to translate not very. For example:

> **Ils sont peu nombreux.**
> [There aren't very many of them.]
> **Il est peu patient.**
> [He's not very patient.]

Rewrite the following sentences, finding an alternative for **pas beaucoup** or **pas très** each time.

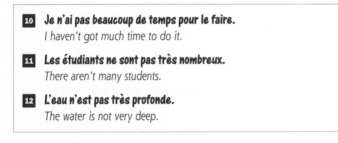

10 Je n'ai pas beaucoup de temps pour le faire.
I haven't got much time to do it.

11 Les étudiants ne sont pas très nombreux.
There aren't many students.

12 L'eau n'est pas très profonde.
The water is not very deep.

II How to translate 'most of'

la majorité de the majority of, most of	**le plus de** (the) most (= more than all the rest), e.g. **C'est lui qui a eu le plus de voix**. He got the most votes.
la plus grosse part de l'argent most (= the greatest part, proportion) of the money	
une bonne partie de a good part of	Alternatively, use **presque tout(e)**, **tous, toutes** (see Day 5, Section II for adjective agreement), e.g.
la majeure partie de most of	**presque tout le temps** – most of the time; **presque tous les étudiants –** most of the students.
la plus grande partie de most of	
la plupart des most of, the majority of	

Fill in the gaps in the following sentences by using an appropriate expression from the list above.

13 Les enfants ont mangé la plus grosse _ _ _ _ _ _ _ _ _ _ _ du gâteau.
The children ate most of the cake.

14 C'est là qu'on a eu le _ _ _ _ _ _ _ _ _ _ de problèmes.
That's what gave us the most trouble.

15 Ils ont entamé une bonne _ _ _ _ _ _ _ _ du capital.
They have eaten into a good part of the capital.

16 Elle passe la _ _ _ _ _ _ _ _ _ _ partie de son temps à lire.
She spends most of her time reading.

17 Pendant la plus grande _ _ _ _ _ _ _ _ _ _ _ de la soirée elle n'a rien dit.
For most of the evening she said nothing.

18 Il travaille _ _ _ _ _ _ _ _ _ _ _ tout le temps.
He works most of the time.

III Other quantifiers
You should also include the following in your active vocabulary.

assez de enough	**chacun de** each of
autant de so many	**une partie de** some of
tant de so many (Note that it is not permissible to say ***si beaucoup**!)	**que de**! what a lot of!
	le reste de the rest/remainder of

Fill in the gaps in the following sentences by using an appropriate expression from the list above.

19 Je ne savais pas que vous aviez _ _ _ _ _ _ _ _ _ de livres.
I didn't know you had so many books.

20 _ _ _ _ _ _ _ _ _ _ de monde!
What a lot of people!

21 Est'ce qu'il y aura _ _ _ _ _ _ _ _ de place?
Will there be enough room?

22 Je vais récupérer le _ _ _ _ _ _ _ _ _ de mes affaires.
I'm going to pick up the rest of my things.

23 _ _ _ _ _ _ _ _ _ d'entre vous est libre de choisir.
Each of you is free to choose.

IV   How to translate 'some'

In addition to the plural indefinite article, **des** (see Day 7), there are a number of other ways of translating 'some', each with a different shade of meaning.

- First, note the difference between **quelques** [some = only a few] and **plusieurs** [several = quite a few].
- If some/several means 'various', then try either **différent(e)s** or **divers(es)**.
- Note the usefulness of **certain** [some = particular], e.g. **un certain temps** [some time]; **dans une certaine mesure** [to some extent]; **certaines personnes** [some people]; **à certains moments** [sometimes]; **certains d'entre nous** [some of us].
- Finally, instead of an adjective, you could try **un certain nombre de**.

Complete the following sentences, translating 'some' or 'several' each time with an appropriate expression from the list above.

24 Vos remarques ont eu un _ _ _ _ _ _ _ _ _ _ _ _ effet.
Your remarks did have some effect.

25 Nous avons attendu _ _ _ _ _ _ _ _ _ _ _ _ _ heures.
We waited for some (= quite a lot of) hours.

26 Je suis d'accord avec toi sur _ _ _ _ _ _ _ _ _ points.
I agree with you on some points.

27 Un _ _ _ _ _ _ _ _ _ _ _ _ _ _ _ _ _ de délégués se sont abstenus.
Some delegates abstained.

28 Il pourrait y avoir _ _ _ _ _ _ _ _ _ _ _ _ explications.
There could be several explanations.

29 _ _ _ _ _ _ _ _ _ _ _ _ _ _ _ _ d'entre eux n'ont pas pu assister à la réunion.
Some of them weren't able to attend the meeting.

30 **Je voudrais ajouter** _ _ _ _ _ _ _ _ **mots.**
I would like to add some (= a few) words.

See for further information
Hawkins and Towell, 6.9
Jubb and Rouxeville, Chapter 14
Judge and Healey, Chapter 12, §2.1.4
Byrne and Churchill §§320–37
Ferrar, §§119, 219, 226–7

I   Conditional clause or indirect question

For most of today you will be focusing on the use of **si** in conditional (or hypothetical) clauses. For example:

> **Si vous comprenez ce paragraphe, vous n'aurez plus de problèmes.**
> [If you understand this paragraph, you won't have any more problems.]

First, however, you need to be able to distinguish between the use of **si** in conditional clauses and the use of **si** to introduce an indirect/reported question. For example:

> **Elle m'a demandé si je pourrais passer plus tard.**
> [She asked me if (= whether) I could call by later.]

The use of tenses in these two cases is quite different and is often confused. If in doubt, there is a simple way of checking whether you are dealing with a conditional clause or a reported question. In a reported question, as in the second example above, **si** can be translated into English as 'if' or as 'whether'. By contrast, in a conditional clause, it can only be translated as 'if'.

Study the following sentences and identify the cases where **si** introduces a conditional clause (C) and the cases where it introduces an indirect question (Q). Mark the sentences (C) or (Q) as appropriate and note the use of tenses in each case.

1   Si j'ai le temps, je lui donnerai un coup de main.
If I have time, I will give her/him a hand.

2   Il m'a demandé si je pourrais lui donner un coup de main.
He asked me if I could give him a hand.

3   Je lui donnerais un coup de main si j'avais le temps.
I would give her/him a hand if I had time.

4   Je ne sais pas si j'aurai le temps de lui donner un coup de main.
I don't know if I will have time to give her/him a hand.

5   Je lui aurais donné un coup de main si j'avais eu le temps.
I would have given her/him a hand if I had had time.

6 **Je ne savais pas si j'aurais le temps de lui donner un coup de main.**
  I didn't know if I would have time to give her/him a hand.

7 **Si vous avez le temps, donnez-lui un coup de main.**
  If you have time, give her/him a hand.

II   Three basic patterns of tense usage

Happily, once you know you are dealing with a conditional clause, the use of tenses in the sentence is quite straightforward. There are three main patterns to follow:

i)   ***Si*** + present tense, followed by future tense in the main clause. For example:

> **Si j'ai le temps, je lui donnerai un coup de main.**
> [If I have time, I will give her/him a hand.]

You will also find the following variants on this pattern:

- ***Si*** + present tense, followed by imperative in the main clause. For example:

> **Si vous avez le temps, donnez-lui un coup de main**.
> [If you have time, give her/him a hand.]

- ***Si*** + present tense, followed by a present tense in the main clause. For example:

> **Si vous avez le temps, vous pouvez lui donner un coup de main.**
> [If you have time, you can give her/him a hand.]

⚠ The one thing which you must never do is to use the future tense in the **si** clause.

ii)   ***Si*** + imperfect, followed by conditional in the main clause. For example:

> **Si j'avais le temps**, **je lui donnerais un coup de main**.
> [If I had time, I would give her/him a hand.]

This pattern is the most problematic, because English tense usage varies in the 'if' clause. So, we might say 'If I did have time', 'If I were to have time', even occasionally 'If I should have time', or simply 'If I had time'. The French imperfect tense translates all of these.

⚠ The one thing you must never do is use the conditional in the **si** clause.

iii)   ***Si*** + pluperfect, followed by past conditional in the main clause. For example:

> **Si j'avais eu le temps, je lui aurais donné un coup de main**.
> [If I had had time, I would have given her/him a hand.]

⚠ The one thing you must never do is use the past conditional in the **si** clause.

Finally, you should note that in all cases the order of the conditional and the main clauses may be reversed. For example:

Je lui aurais donné un coup de main si j'avais eu le temps.
[I would have given her/him a hand if I had had time.]

But the pattern of tense usage still remains the same.

One other small thing to note: **si** + **il(s)** elides to **s'il(s)**, but **si** + **elle(s)** remains unchanged.

Put the verbs in the following sentences into the appropriate tense.

---

8 Si vous le _ _ _ _ _ (voir) demain, dites-lui bonjour de ma part.
If you see him tomorrow, give him my regards.

9 Je vous aurais invité si je _ _ _ _ _ _ _ _ (savoir) que vous étiez là.
I would have invited you if I had known that you were there.

10 Si nous _ _ _ _ _ _ _ (arriver) avant minuit, nous vous donnerons un coup de fil.
If we arrive before midnight, we will give you a ring.

11 Elle a dit que s'il lui _ _ _ _ _ _ _ (téléphoner) elle raccrocherait tout de suite.
She said that if he phoned her she would hang up straightaway.

Correct the errors in the sentences below.

---

12 Elle a dit que si elle serait fatiguée, elle ferait la sieste.
She said that if she was tired, she would have a nap.

13 Si nous aurons le temps, nous passerons les voir.
If we have time, we will call to see them.

14 S'il aurait lu ce texte, il aurait tout compris.
If he had read this text, he would have understood everything.

On Day 23 you will be looking more closely at modal verbs (**pouvoir**, **devoir**), but note here the particular difficulty in rendering English 'could' into French. It may help if you paraphrase 'could' before you translate as either 'was/were able to' (= imperfect) or as 'would be able to' (= conditional) as appropriate. For example:

Si vous pouviez me donner ses coordonnées, je pourrais l'ajouter à notre fichier-clientèle.
[If you could (were able to) give me his contact details, I could (would be able to) add him to our mailing list.]

But if you follow the rules for use of tenses in conditional sentences, all should be well anyway!

Complete the sentences below with the appropriate tense of **pouvoir**.

---

15   **Si je _ _ _ _ _ _ vous aider, je le ferais volontiers.**
If I could help you, I would willingly do so.

16   **Si elle avait plus d'argent, elle _ _ _ _ _ _ _ s'acheter une voiture.**
If she had more money, she could buy herself a car.

17   **Ils _ _ _ _ _ _ _ _ _ _ aller à Paris s'ils en avaient vraiment envie.**
They could go to Paris if they really wanted to.

18   **S'ils _ _ _ _ _ _ _ _ _ _ partir, ils iraient aux Etats-Unis.**
If they could leave, they would go to the United States.

III   One further pattern of tense usage

The one other main pattern of tense usage to note is the following.

Si + passé composé, followed by present, future or passé composé in the main clause. For example:

> **Si je me suis trompé, je suis désolé.**
> [If I have made a mistake, I am sorry.]
> **S'il a manqué son train, il sera furieux.**
> [If he has missed his train, he will be furious.]
> **Si j'ai bien compris, vous avez perdu votre billet.**
> [If I have understood correctly, you have lost your ticket.]

⚠ Note that the passé composé corresponds here to the English perfect, 'If he has missed his train'. Don't be tempted to use the passé composé after **si** when dealing with sentences which follow pattern ii (see Section II above). For example:

> **S'il manquait son train, il serait furieux**.
> [If he missed (were to miss) his train, he would be furious.]

Choose the appropriate tense to fill the gap in each of the sentences below.

---

19   **S'il manquait/a manqué le rendez-vous, il ne l'a pas fait exprès.**
If he missed the appointment, he did not do so on purpose.

20   **S'il partait/est parti, je sais qu'il nous aura laissé un mot.**
If he has left, I know that he will have left us a message.

21   **S'il partait/est parti, il essayerait de nous faire signe.**
If he were leaving, he would try to contact us.

IV   Final reminder

* The most commonly used tenses after **si** in conditional clauses are the present, the imperfect, the pluperfect. More rarely, you may find the passé composé.
* The tenses which you should *never* use after **si** in conditional clauses are the future, the future perfect, the conditional, and the past conditional.

Correct the underlined errors in the following sentences written by students.

---

22 S'il y a *eu* plus de pistes cyclables, nos enfants pourraient aller à l'école à bicyclette.
If there were more cycle lanes, our children could cycle to school.

23 S'ils n'étaient pas aussi riches, prenait-on au sérieux leurs arguments?
If they were not so rich, would their arguments be taken seriously?

24 Si l'on *pourrait* trouver son dossier, peut-être pourrait-on résoudre le problème.
If they could find his file, perhaps they could solve the problem.

25 Sa situation *changera* si elle était enceinte.
Her position would change if she were pregnant.

26 S'il n'y *aurait* pas de discrimination, nous n'aurions pas besoin d'avoir une guerre des sexes.
If there were no discrimination, we would not need a war between the sexes.

IV   Ring the changes or avoid the problem!

It is sometimes possible to express a condition by using **en cas de**, **avec** or **sans** + a noun. For example:

> **Sans aide, il ne s'en sortira jamais.**
> [Without help (If he does not have help), he will never cope.]
> **En cas de difficultés, adressez-vous à la concierge.**
> [In the event of problems (If you have problems), apply to the caretaker.]

Try your hand at rewriting the following sentences, replacing **si** + verb by one of these constructions.

---

27 Si l'on n'a pas de domicile fixe, il est difficile de trouver un emploi.
If you have no fixed address, it is difficult to find a job.

28 S'il y a un incendie, brisez la glace.
If there is a fire, break the glass.

29   *Si vous tombez en panne, réfugiez-vous sur la bande d'arrêt d'urgence.*
If you break down, take refuge on the hard shoulder.

30   *Ils ont dit que s'ils avaient un peu de chance ils pourraient nous rejoindre plus tard.*
They said that if they were lucky they might be able to join us later.

See for further information

Hawkins and Towell, 10.8
Jubb and Rouxeville, Chapter 7
Judge and Healey, Chapter 6, §3.4
Byrne and Churchill, §§415–24
Ferrar, §22

Do you find that you sometimes make mistakes with words which look very similar in English and French, but which have different meanings? Do you sometimes misspell French words which are slightly different from their English look-alikes? The exercises which follow are designed to help you to be aware of these sorts of error and either to avoid them in the first place or to pick them up and correct them when you check over your work.

I Deceptive look-alikes

Note the following **faux amis** – French words which look very similar to English words, but which have a different meaning – and note also how you should translate the English look-alike words into French. The asterisked items are further illustrated in example sentences at the end of the list.

Faux ami	English equivalent	English look-alike	French translation
achèvement (m)	completion	achievement	**accomplissement** (m), **exploit** (m)
achever	to complete, finish off	to achieve	**accomplir**
actuellement	at present	actually	**en fait**
change (m)	exchange	change	**changement** (m)
***caractère** (m)	character (= personality/ nature)	character (= in a play/ novel; individual)	***personnage** (m)
conférence (f)	lecture	conference	**congrès** (m)
délai (m)	time allowed	delay	**retard** (m)
***demander**	to ask for	demand	***exiger**
effectif	real, actual	effective	**efficace**
éventuellement	possibly	eventually	**finalement**
***évidence** (f)	obviousness, fact	evidence	***témoignage** (m)
(Note the adjective **évident** means obvious.)			
issue (f)	exit; outcome	issue	**problème**
passer un examen	to sit an exam	to pass an exam	**être reçu à un examen**
partie (f)	part	party (political)	**parti** (m)
procès (m)	trial, lawsuit	process	**processus** (m)

i) **caractère/personnage** [character]
    Il a du caractère.
    [He has character]
    Ce n'est pas dans son caractère de s'imposer.
    [It's not in her/his nature to make her/his presence felt.]
    Les personnages de ce roman sont peu convaincants.
    [The characters in this novel are not very convincing.]

ii) **demander/exiger** [ask for/demand]
    Il a demandé de l'argent à son père.
    [He asked his father for money.]
    Il a exigé qu'ils partent tout de suite.
    [He demanded that they leave straightaway.]
    Note also that you must use the verb **poser** when translating 'to ask a
    question', e.g. **Le journaliste a posé des questions indiscrètes.** [The
    journalist asked intrusive questions.]

iii) **évidence/témoignage** [evidence]
     C'est l'évidence même.
     [It's glaringly obvious.]
     J'ai laissé les clefs bien en évidence sur son bureau.
     [I left the keys in an obvious place on his desk.]
     **Les témoignages recueillis auprès des victimes sont
     contradictoires.**
     [The evidence given by the victims is contradictory.]

Read the following sentences and first underline the words which have been used
in error in the context. Then choose from the alphabetical list below the
word/expression which should have been used in each sentence and rewrite the
sentences with the replacement words in the correct form.

l'accomplissement/l'exploit, le changement, le congrès, efficace, en
fait, exiger, finalement, le parti, le personnage, poser, le problème, le
processus, être reçu à, le retard, le témoignage

1 **Les issues dont on discute sont très complexes.**
    The issues under discussion are very complicated.

2 **Les parties politiques prennent position sur ce problème.**
    The political parties are taking a stand on this issue.

3 **Ces plantes demandent des soins constants.**
    These plants require constant care.

4 **Il leur demande des questions trop difficiles.**
He asks them questions which are too difficult.

5 **Le procès de paix est très délicat.**
The peace process is very delicate.

6 **Cet acteur sait vraiment se mettre dans la peau de son caractère.**
This actor really knows how to get inside the character.

7 **C'est un achèvement formidable.**
It's a wonderful achievement.

8 – 9 **Eventuellement le train est arrivé avec deux heures de délai.**
Eventually the train arrived two hours late.

10 **La police a entendu l'évidence de son voisin de palier.**
The police heard the evidence of his neighbour on the same floor.

11 **La conférence se déroulera à Montréal du 3 au 5 avril.**
The conference will take place in Montreal from 3 to 5 April.

12 **Le change de stratégie les a beaucoup surpris.**
The change in strategy has greatly surprised them.

13 **Je le croyais dangereux, mais actuellement c'est un bon conducteur.**
I thought he was dangerous, but actually he is a good driver.

14 **Il a mené une campagne très effective.**
He has led a very effective campaign.

15 **Il faut obtenir une note d'au moins 9 sur 20 pour passer l'examen.**
You must get a mark of at least 9 out of 20 to pass the exam.

Check that you are really confident of the different meanings by completing the following sentences with the appropriate word chosen from the alternatives given in brackets.

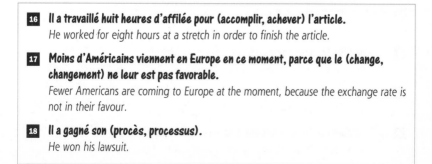

16 **Il a travaillé huit heures d'affilée pour (accomplir, achever) l'article.**
He worked for eight hours at a stretch in order to finish the article.

17 **Moins d'Américains viennent en Europe en ce moment, parce que le (change, changement) ne leur est pas favorable.**
Fewer Americans are coming to Europe at the moment, because the exchange rate is not in their favour.

18 **Il a gagné son (procès, processus).**
He won his lawsuit.

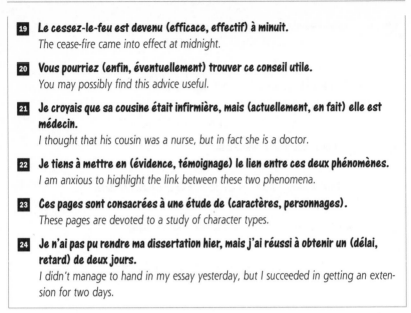

19 **Le cessez-le-feu est devenu (efficace, effectif) à minuit.**
The cease-fire came into effect at midnight.

20 **Vous pourriez (enfin, éventuellement) trouver ce conseil utile.**
You may possibly find this advice useful.

21 **Je croyais que sa cousine était infirmière, mais (actuellement, en fait) elle est médecin.**
I thought that his cousin was a nurse, but in fact she is a doctor.

22 **Je tiens à mettre en (évidence, témoignage) le lien entre ces deux phénomènes.**
I am anxious to highlight the link between these two phenomena.

23 **Ces pages sont consacrées à une étude de (caractères, personnages).**
These pages are devoted to a study of character types.

24 **Je n'ai pas pu rendre ma dissertation hier, mais j'ai réussi à obtenir un (délai, retard) de deux jours.**
I didn't manage to hand in my essay yesterday, but I succeeded in getting an extension for two days.

This has practised just a few of the most common problem words. Always be on your guard and check in your dictionary if you are in any doubt.

II   Spelling problems

You may find that you hesitate over spelling some English words after having learnt their French counterparts, e.g. depend*ent* (adj.) in English, but **dépend*ant*** in French, respons*i*ble in English, but **respons*a*ble** in French. More commonly, perhaps, you may need to check your French spelling to make sure that it is free from English influence.

Check the following sentences. Tick any which you think are all right, and correct any misspellings which you find.

25 **Prenons un example au hasard.**
Let's take an example at random.

26 **C'est un artiste sensationel.**
He is a fantastic artist.

27 **Il parle d'un ton très aggressif.**
He speaks in a very aggressive way.

28 **Il est parti sans laisser d'adresse.**
He left without leaving an address.

29 **Il s'est donné pour objective d'écrire deux mille mots par jour.**
He set himself the goal of writing two thousand words per day.

You should have made four corrections. Watch out for similar problems, particularly with single/double consonants, in future.

Look again at sentence 29 above. Did you confuse the feminine form of the adjective, **objectif, objective**, with the noun **un objectif**? Can you spot and correct a similar error in the sentence below?

---

30 *Ce livre s'adresse à une publique jeune.*
This book is aimed at a young audience.

Finally, make sure you avoid the common misspelling of *__beacoup__ for **bea*u*coup**! Remember the link with the adjective **beau**.

Key points:
Past tenses

Today you will be concentrating on points of tense formation that are amenable to correction in a short revision programme of this kind. If the larger question of when to use the imperfect, when the passé composé and when the past historic bothers you, consult the reference grammars listed on p. 70.

I Choosing between *avoir* and *être*

The difficulty is remembering the minority of verbs which form the passé composé, pluperfect and other compound tenses with the auxiliary **être**.

All pronominal/reflexive verbs do so (see Day 14). For example:

> **Il s'est endormi.**
> [He fell asleep.]
> **Elle s'est souvenue de la date.**
> [She remembered the date.]

There are 13 common verbs, mostly verbs of motion, which also do so. For example:

> **Il est arrivé.**
> [He arrived.]

It helps to learn them in the following pairs of antonyms (opposites): **aller**, **venir**; **arriver**, **partir**; **descendre**, **monter**; **entrer**, **sortir**; **naître**, **mourir**. There are three others to remember: **rester**, **retourner**, **tomber**.

Don't forget that compounds of the above verbs, e.g. **devenir**, **survenir**, **advenir**, **rentrer**, **repartir**, **ressortir**, **etc**. also take **être**. For example:

> **Elle est devenue très acariâtre.**
> [She became very cantankerous.]

Rewrite the following sentences in the passé composé.

---

1 **Nous retournons dans notre pays natal.**
We are returning (have returned) to our native country.

2 **Qu'est-ce qu'il devient?**
What is he up to? (What has become of him?)

3 **Il survient une difficulté inattendue.**
An unexpected difficulty arises (has arisen).

4 **Ils ressortent par la porte de derrière.**
They're going out again (have gone out again) by the back door.

Do you sometimes make the mistake of trying to form the past tenses of **avoir** or **être** with **être**? Both verbs take the auxiliary **avoir**.

Complete the following sentences with the correct form of the passé composé of either **avoir** or **être** as indicated.

5 **J' _ _ _ _ _ _ _ _ ce livre pour cinquante francs. (avoir)**
I got this book for fifty francs.

6 **L'élection _ _ _ _ _ _ _ _ sans surprise. (être)**
The election went as expected.

7 **Ils _ _ _ _ _ _ _ _ _ contents de leur séjour. (être)**
They were pleased with their stay.

II   Formation of past participles

- There are a number of irregular past participles to learn, e.g. **être** > **été**; **avoir** > **eu**; **faire** > **fait; recevoir** > **reçu; asseoir** > **assis; mettre** > **mis; prendre** > **pris; lire** > **lu**; **venir** > **venu**; **mourir** > **mort**; **craindre** > **craint**.
- Again, watch out particularly for compounds of these verbs, e.g. **satisfaire** > **satisfait; surprendre** > **surpris; devenir** > **devenu** and verbs belonging to irregular families, e.g. verbs ending in -**evoir**: **recevoir, apercevoir**; verbs ending in -**ndre**: **craindre, joindre, peindre**.
- Students sometimes make a slip with the past participle of regular -**ir** verbs. Note that this form ends in -**i**, e.g. **finir** > **fini**. Don't be tempted to write **finit**. That is the third-person singlar present indicative and past historic form!

Rewrite the following sentences in the passé composé.

8 **Je m'aperçois d'une erreur.**
I notice (have noticed) a mistake.

9 **Il choisit de ne pas répondre.**
He chooses (has chosen) not to reply.

10 **Ces enfants apprennent à nager.**
These children are learning (have learnt) to swim.

11 **Ils se joignent à la foule.**
They are joining (have joined) the crowd.

Note: See Day 13 for the agreement of past participles.

III *Il y a*

Students often forget that **il y a** [there is] is formed from the infinitive (**y**) **avoir** and not from **être**. The passé composé and pluperfect forms are **il y a eu** [there has been] and **il y avait eu** [there had been]. Two points to watch:

- Don't use the past participle of **être**, **été**, by mistake!
- Use the auxiliary **avoir**, not **être**.

Note that the passé composé or the past historic and not the imperfect translates 'there was/were' when a completed event (often a sudden happening) is involved. For example:

> **Il y a eu un coup de tonnerre.**
> [There was a clap of thunder.]

Correct the errors in the following sentences.

12 **Il n'y a jamais été de phénomène pareil.**
There has never been such a phenomenon.

13 **S'il n'y était pas eu de guerre, nous ne nous serions jamais rencontrés.**
If there had not been a war, we would never have met.

14 **Il y a était une explosion sociale.**
There was a social outcry.

15 **Il ne savait pas qu'il y avait été une catastrophe.**
He didn't know that there had been a catastrophe.

IV Formation and meaning of pluperfect

The pluperfect, formed from the imperfect of **avoir** or **être** and the past participle, e.g. **j'avais mangé**, translates both 'I had eaten' and 'I had been eating'. It is often found in reported speech (see Day 2) and after **si** in conditional sentences (see Day 9).

The most common errors to watch are:

- Choosing the wrong auxiliary, **avoir** instead of **être** or vice versa (see Section I above).

- Using the passé composé or past historic of **avoir/être** instead of the imperfect. If you do this you will have either a **passé surcomposé** or a past anterior. These tenses are only used in very particular circumstances (see reference grammars listed at the end of this unit).
- Trying to translate the progressive 'had been eating' with *j'avais été + a present or past participle. It is rarely necessary to express the ongoing nature of the activity, but if it is, use **j'avais été en train de manger** [I had been eating] (cf. Day 3, Section VI).

Correct the errors in the following sentences.

---

16 **Elle ne savait pas qu'il avait déjà arrivé.**
She didn't know that he had already arrived.

17 **Il se rendit compte qu'elle eut manqué le train.**
He realized that she had missed the train.

18 **Il l'invita à entrer et l'accompagna jusqu'au salon, où il avait été travaillant.**
He invited her to come in and took her into the living room where he had been working.

19 **Pendant son absence à l'étranger, ses petits-enfants ont été beaucoup grandi.**
During his absence abroad, his grandchildren had grown up a great deal.

20 **Ils avaient été bu trop de bière.**
They had been drinking too much beer.

V   Tenses with *depuis* and *venir de*

Remember to use the present tense in French where English uses a perfect in the following cases:

- to translate 'to have just done something', use the present tense of **venir** + **de** + infinitive. For example:

Je viens d'acheter un nouveau CD.
[I have just bought a new CD.]

- to express an action which began in the past but which is still continuing in the present. For example:

Nous habitons ici depuis cinq ans.
[We have been living here for five years.]
Il y a cinq ans que nous habitons ici.
[We have been living here for five years.]
Voilà cinq ans que nous habitons ici.
[We have been living here for five years.]
Ça fait cinq ans que nous habitons ici.
[We have been living here for five years.]

Complete the following sentences, using a present tense verb form in each case.

---

21 Ils ne _ _ _ _ _ _ _ _ _ _ _ _ _ _ _ que d'emménager.
They have only just moved in.

22 Ça fait quinze jours que je _ _ _ _ _ _ _ _ _ à ce rapport.
I've been working on this report for a fortnight.

23 Est-ce que vous savez depuis combien de temps il _ _ _ _ _ _ _ _ à cette univer-sité?
Do you know how long he has been studying at this university?

24 Ils la _ _ _ _ _ _ _ _ _ _ _ depuis des années.
They have known her for years.

Similarly, remember in the same circumstances to use an imperfect in French where English uses a pluperfect. For example:

> **Je ne savais pas que sa femme venait de mourir.**
> [I didn't know his wife had just died.]
> **Elle nous a expliqué que son fils travaillait en Amérique depuis quatre ans.**
> [She explained to us that her son had been working in America for four years.]

The imperfect is used here with **depuis** to refer to an action which had begun earlier, but which was still continuing at the time of speaking.

Complete the following sentences, using an imperfect tense verb form in each case.

---

25 Est-ce que vous saviez qu'il _ _ _ _ _ _ _ _ _ ici depuis si longtemps?
Did you know that he had been living here so long?

26 Elle ne _ _ _ _ _ _ _ _ _ _ _ que d'entendre la nouvelle quand elle m'a téléphoné.
She had only just heard the news when she phoned me.

See also Day 12, Section II for the translation of 'for' + an expression of time into French. Finally, to revise this whole unit, correct the errors in the following sentences.

---

27 Il avait finit son travail.
He had finished his work.

28 Elle ne savait pas qu'il avait mouru.
She didn't know that he had died.

29 **Il y a été un incendie.**
There had been a fire.

30 **L'avion est venu d'atterrir.**
The plane has just landed.

See for further information
Hawkins and Towell, Chapters 7, 10
Jubb and Rouxeville, Chapters 2, 3, 4, 5
Judge and Healey, Chapters 4, 10
Byrne and Churchill, §§348–78
Ferrar, §§1–12, 15–19

Do you have problems translating the word 'time' into French? There are a number of different words, each with a particular range of meanings. Study the examples below to refresh your memory.

I   Time itself

i) **FOIS** (f) occasion
une fois, deux fois, trois fois once, twice, three times

cette fois this time	**la première fois** the first time
parfois at times	**la dernière fois** the last time
quelquefois sometimes	**encore une fois** once again

une autre fois another time; next time
Also note the following expressions:
à la fois at the same time; both, e.g. **Ne parlez pas tous à la fois.** Don't all speak at once.
C'est difficile et ennuyeux à la fois. It's both (at one and the same time) difficult and boring.
Il y avait une fois Once upon a time there was

ii) **INSTANT, MOMENT** point in time
à cet instant-là; à ce moment-là at that time (then)
en ce moment at this time (now)
au bon/mauvais moment at the right/wrong time/moment
au même moment at the same time

iii) **TEMPS** (Note that **temps** ends in **-s** in the singular and in the plural.)
   a) length of time; time as a general phenomenon
   le temps passe vite time flies
   avoir le temps de faire quelque chose to have time to do something
   tout le temps (for) the whole time
   longtemps (for) a long time
   b) right time for
   arriver à temps pour to arrive in time

c) period (usually in the past)
dans le temps in days gone by
en ce temps-là at that time, in those days
en même temps at the same time
en temps de guerre/paix in wartime/peacetime

iv) **HEURE** time relating to hour of the day
Quelle heure est-il? What time is it?
l'heure d'un rendez-vous the time of an appointment
les heures de bureau/de classe office hours/school hours
les heures d'ouverture/de fermeture opening/closing times
à l'heure on time

v) **EPOQUE** (f) period, age
à cette époque at that time
à l'époque où at the time when
à l'époque de Louis XIV in the time of Louis XIV

vi) **DELAI** (m) period of time allowed; deadline
dans les délais convenus within the agreed time
demander un délai to ask for extra time

Fill in the gaps in the following sentences using an appropriate expression from the list above.

1 **Je vais à la piscine** _ _ _ _ _ _ _ _ _ _ _ _ _ **par semaine.**
I go to the swimming pool once a week.

2 **On ne devrait pas faire cela pendant** _ _ _ _ _ _ _ _ _ _ _ _ _ _ _ _ _ **du bureau.**
You shouldn't do that in company time.

3 **Il faut** _ _ _ _ _ _ _ _ _ _ _ _ _ _ _ **pour apprendre une langue.**
It takes time to learn a language.

4 _ **peu de gens savaient lire.**
At that time (= in those days) few people could read.

5 **Ils sont arrivés** _ _ _ _ _ _ _ _ _ _ _ _ _ _ _ _ _ _ _ **pour le début de la séance.**
They arrived in time for the beginning of the film.

6 **Elle est** _ _ _ _ _ _ _ _ _ _ _ **irritable.**
She is sometimes short-tempered.

7 **C'est le bon** _ _ _ _ _ _ _ _ _ _ _ _ _ _ **pour commencer.**
It's a good time to start.

8 **Elle est tout** _ **gouvernante, infirmière et secrétaire.**
She is at one and the same time housekeeper, nurse and secretary.

9 **Il a terminé le rapport dans** _.
He finished the report within the agreed time.

10 **Nous habitons ici depuis** _ _ _ _ _ _ _ _ _ _ _.
We have lived here for a long time.

II Prepositions with expressions of time

The first problem is how to translate 'for' with an expression of time. **Pour** is used for intended periods of time, often in the future. For example:

> **Je vais à Paris pour un mois.**
> [I'm going to Paris for a month.]

But **pour** is not usually needed with the verb **rester**. For example:

> **Elle va rester six mois à Paris.**
> [She's going to stay for six months in Paris.]

Pendant is used for actual periods of time, past, present or future. For example:

> **Je l'ai attendu pendant des heures.**
> [I waited for him for hours.]
> **Elle travaille à la bibliothèque pendant toute la durée des vacances.**
> [She's working in the library for the entire vacation.]
> **Nous allons travailler ici pendant trois mois.**
> [We're going to work here for three months.]

But **pendant** is not usually needed with the verb **rester**. For example:

> **Elle est restée trois heures à bavarder.**
> [She stayed for three hours chatting.]

Depuis is used for a period of time up to a present or past moment (see Day 11, Section V). For example:

> **Nous habitons ici depuis trois ans.**
> [We have lived here for three years.]
> **Il habitait l'appartement depuis six mois.**
> [He had lived in the flat for six months.]

Fill in the gaps in the following sentences with one of the prepositions (**pour, pendant, depuis**), or leave with no preposition as appropriate.

11 **Il apprenait le français** _ _ _ _ _ _ **deux ans quand il s'est installé à Paris.**
He had been learning French for two years when he moved to Paris.

12 **J'ai hésité** _ _ _ _ _ _ _ _ _ **quelques instants.**
I hesitated for a few moments.

13 **Restez** _ _ _ _ _ _ _ _ **un moment.**
Stay for a little while.

14 **Nous allons à Londres** _ _ _ _ _ _ _ **le weekend.**
We're going to London for the weekend.

The second problem is how to translate 'in' with an expression of time. **En** is used to indicate the length of time which something takes. For example:

J'ai terminé le rapport en une heure.
[I finished the report in an hour.]

Dans is used for a deadline, when 'in' means 'time at the end of which'. For example:

Ils seront de retour dans une heure.
[They'll be back in an hour.]

Fill in the gaps in the following sentences with **en** or **dans** as appropriate.

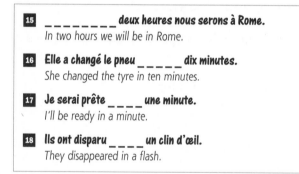

15 _ _ _ _ _ _ _ _ **deux heures nous serons à Rome.**
In two hours we will be in Rome.

16 **Elle a changé le pneu** _ _ _ _ _ _ **dix minutes.**
She changed the tyre in ten minutes.

17 **Je serai prête** _ _ _ _ **une minute.**
I'll be ready in a minute.

18 **Ils ont disparu** _ _ _ _ **un clin d'œil.**
They disappeared in a flash.

III   Year, day, morning, evening

Do you have difficulty deciding whether to use **an**, **jour**, **matin**, **soir** or the feminine forms **année**, **journée**, **matinée**, **soirée**? Remember the following as a rule of thumb:

• Use the masculine forms after cardinal numbers.

Nous sommes restés trois ans.
[We stayed for three years.]

• Use the feminine forms after ordinal numbers and indefinites.

Elle est étudiante en deuxième année.
[She's a second-year student.]
En quelques années elle a fait beaucoup de progrès.
[Within the space of a few years she has made a lot of progress.]

But you will find that this does not work in all cases. The distinction is often one of style, with the feminine form emphasizing the length of time, or the events that take place within it. For example:

Il a eu trois années difficiles à l'université.
[He had three difficult years at university.]
Ces cinq dernières années il a beaucoup vieilli.
[He has aged a lot in the last five years.]

And, more generally, this emphasis on length of time or the events that take place within it is what determines the use of the feminine form. For example:

J'ai travaillé pendant toute la matinée/journée/soirée.
[I worked all morning/day/evening.]

Sometimes, though, it is purely a matter of convention. Note the following set phrases.

---

en début de matinée/soirée/ journée at the beginning of the morning/evening/day
en fin de matinée/soirée/journée at the end of the morning/ evening/day

les années 80 the eighties
l'année précédente/suivante the previous/following year

Complete the following sentences with the appropriate masculine or feminine form, making any adjectives agree as necessary.

19 Les _ _ _ _ _ _ _ _ _ _ _ commencent à s'allonger.
The days are beginning to lengthen.

20 Elle est en premier/première _ _ _ _ _ _ _ _ _ _ _ _ de DEUG.
She's in the first year of her DEUG.

21 Cela représente tout un/une _ _ _ _ _ _ _ _ _ _ _ de travail.
That represents a whole morning's work.

22 La réunion se déroule le/la _ _ _ _ _ _ _ _ _ _ _.
The meeting is taking place in the morning.

23 Je les ai vus en début de _ _ _ _ _ _ _ _ _ _.
I saw them at the beginning of the evening.

24 Dans quelques _ _ _ _ _ _ _ _ elle aura tout oublié.
In a few years' time she will have forgotten all about it.

25 *Je les ai connus dans les* _ _ _ _ _ _ _ _ _ _ *soixante-dix.*
I met them in the seventies.

26 *Il prendra sa retraite dans deux* _ _ _ _ _ .
He will retire in two years' time.

IV   Le lendemain, la veille

Remember the very useful words, **le lendemain** (the following day), and **la veille** (the day before) and note the following expressions.

le lendemain de l'accident the day after the accident	**la veille au soir** the night/evening before
le lendemain matin/soir the following morning/evening	**la veille de son départ** the day before he left
du jour au lendemain from one day to the next	**à la veille de** on the eve of
au lendemain de la guerre just after the war	

Fill in the gaps in the following sentences using an appropriate expression from the list above.

27 *Ils se sont rencontrés* _ _ _ _ _ _ _ _ _ _ _ _ _ _ _ _ _ .
They met the night before.

28 *On ne sait jamais ce qui va se passer* _ .
You never know what's going to happen from one day to the next.

29 *Cette association a été fondée* _ .
This organization was founded just after the war.

30 *Elle est tombée malade* _ _ _ _ _ _ _ _ _ _ _ _ _ _ *de l'examen.*
She fell ill the day before the exam.

See for further information

Hawkins and Towell, 5.6.8–5.6.15
Jubb and Rouxeville, Chapter 26
Judge and Healey, Chapter 12, §5.2
Byrne and Churchill, §§706–12
Ferrar, Appendix C, Time

*A lot of students lose marks for forgetting to make past participles agree or for making them agree when they shouldn't! You saw on Day 5 that when they are used as adjectives they agree with the noun which they qualify. You will be concentrating here on past participles used with **avoir** or **être** to form compound tenses (see Day 11). The agreement of the past participle in passive constructions will be covered on Day 15.*

I   With *avoir*

First, make sure that you don't make past participles agree with the subject of verbs which take the auxiliary **avoir.** This is a very common mistake, so be on your guard. For example:

> **Etes-vous sûrs que vous avez vu ces gens?**
> [Are you sure that you saw those people?]

The past participle **vu** does not agree with the plural subject, **vous**. Nor does it agree with the direct object, **ces gens**, which follows the verb.

If there is a direct object which precedes the verb, then you need to make the past participle agree with that object. For example:

> **Où est la lettre que j'ai reçue ce matin?**
> [Where is the letter which I received this morning?]
> **Je les ai vus hier.**
> [I saw them yesterday.]
> **Quels musées avez-vous visités?**
> [Which museums did you visit?]

Read the following sentences, and decide in each case whether you need to make any change to the ending of the past participle.

---

1   **Les cambrioleurs ont forcé le patron à ouvrir la caisse.**
   The burglars forced the boss to open the till.

2   **Les écologistes nous ont averti de «l'effet de serre».**
   Ecologists have warned us about 'the greenhouse effect'.

---

3 **Je ne trouve pas les documents qu'elle m'a apporté ce matin.**
I can't find the papers which she brought me this morning.

4 **Quelle idée de les avoir invité ce soir!**
How silly to have invited them this evening!

5 **Le système nous a donné ce droit.**
The system has given us this right.

Did you have a problem with number 5? There is an object pronoun, **nous**, before the verb, but it is an indirect object. **On donne un droit** (direct object) **à quelqu'un** (indirect object). With a preceding indirect object, the past participle does not agree. For example:

> **Il nous a parlé.**
> [He spoke to us.]
> **Elle nous a dit au revoir.**
> [She said goodbye to us.]

If in doubt whether you have a direct or indirect object, ask yourself whether a noun used with the verb in question would be preceded by the preposition **à** (indirect object) or no preposition (direct object). In these examples, since you say **parler à une personne** and **dire au revoir à une personne**, you know that an indirect object pronoun is involved.

Choose between the alternative past participle forms given in brackets. If you are unsure whether the pronoun which precedes the verb is a direct or an indirect object, check in the dictionary to see whether the verb in question takes **à** + person or not.

6 **Cette date nous aurait bien (convenu/convenus).**
This date would have suited us well.

7 **Il les a (persuadé/persuadés) d'assister à la réunion.**
He persuaded them to attend the meeting.

8 **Le spectacle nous a beaucoup (plu/plus).**
We enjoyed the show very much.

9 **Je les ai (aidé/aidés) à faire les mots croisés.**
I helped them to do the crosswords.

10 **Il nous a (téléphoné/téléphonés) hier soir.**
He rang us last night.

II With *être*

Look back at Day 11, Section I for the list of verbs which take the auxiliary **être** and remember always to make their past participle agree with the subject. For example:

> **Elle est partie ce matin.**
> [She left this morning.]
> **Ils sont restés à l'hôtel.**
> [They stayed in the hotel.]
> **Elle est tombée dans la rue.**
> [She fell in the street.]

Rewrite the following sentences in the passé composé.

---

11 **La concurrence devient intense.**
The competition is becoming (has become) intense.

12 **Le Président et le Premier Ministre parviennent à un accord.**
The President and the Prime Minister are reaching (have reached) an agreement.

13 **Nous repartons sur de nouvelles bases.**
We are starting (have started) all over again.

III Pronominal and reflexive verbs

With true reflexive verbs, the past participle agrees with the preceding reflexive pronoun, provided that it is the direct object. For example:

> **Elle s'est lavée.**
> [She got washed.]
> **Ils se sont baignés.**
> [They had a swim.]

But watch out for cases where the reflexive pronoun is the indirect object. For example:

> **Elle s'est lavé les mains.**
> [She washed her hands. (= She washed the hands to herself.)]

Here the direct object is **les mains** and it follows the verb, so no agreement. In the following example, the past participle does not agree either.

> **Elle s'est payé un voyage en Chine.**
> [She treated herself to a trip to China.]

This is because the construction is: **payer quelque chose à quelqu'un** [to buy something for someone]. Hence the direct object is **un voyage** and the reflexive pronoun which precedes the verb is the indirect object.

Choose between the alternatives given in brackets. In each case ask yourself whether the pronoun which precedes the verb is a direct or an indirect object. If it is direct, there will be an agreement; if it is indirect, there will not.

14 **Elle s'est (lavé/lavée) les cheveux.**
She washed her hair.

15 **Elle s'est (promis/promise) un weekend à Londres.**
She promised herself a weekend in London.

16 **Elles se sont (servi/servies) les premières.**
They helped themselves first.

17 **Elle s'est (foulé/foulée) la cheville.**
She sprained her ankle.

You need to ask yourself the same question – is the pronoun a direct or indirect object? – when you have a reciprocal action involving two or more people. For example:

Ils se sont rencontrés hier.
[They met (one another) yesterday.]

Here the past participle, **rencontrés**, agrees with **se**, which is the preceding direct object. However, in the next example, the past participle does not agree, because **se** is the indirect object:

Ils se sont parlé au téléphone.
[They spoke to one another on the phone.]

Read the following sentences, and decide in each case whether you need to make any change to the ending of the past participle.

18 **Ils se sont serré la main.**
They shook hands.

19 **Ils se sont aidé à faire leurs devoirs.**
They helped one another to do their homework.

20 **Elles se sont promis de garder le secret.**
They promised one another that they would keep the secret.

21 **Ils se sont écrit tous les jours.**
They wrote to one another every day.

22 **Ils se sont fait beaucoup de mal.**
They have done one another a lot of harm.

That leaves quite a lot of pronominal verbs where the pronoun does not have any reflexive or reciprocal meaning, but is just part of the verb, e.g. **s'apercevoir**, **s'évanouir, se souvenir, se taire**. With these verbs, the past participle agrees with the subject. For example:

Elle s'est évanouie.
[She fainted.]
Ils se sont aperçus de l'erreur.
[They noticed the mistake.]
Ils se sont tus.
[They kept quiet.]

IV   General review
Make the past participles agree as and when necessary. This exercise contains a mixture of verbs – true reflexive, reciprocal, and pronominal with no reflexive/recip-rocal meaning – so be careful! Put together all that you have been practising in this section.

---

23 **Quand est-ce qu'elle s'est (mis/mise) à tousser?**
When did she start coughing?

24 **Ils se sont (posé/posés) la même question.**
They asked themselves the same question.

25 **Les femmes se sont (battu/battues) pour gagner le droit de vote.**
Women fought to gain the right to vote.

26 **Elle s'est (moqué/moquée) de lui.**
She made fun of him.

27 **Ils se sont (envoyé/envoyés) leurs vœux pour la nouvelle année.**
They sent one another New Year's greetings.

Finally, you will sometimes find a preceding direct object used in conjunction with a pronominal verb. For example:

Voici les lettres qu'ils se sont écrites.
[Here are the letters which they wrote to one another.]

In this case, the past participle agrees with **les lettres**, which is the preceding direct object.

Read the following sentences, and decide in each case whether you need to make any change to the ending of the past participle.

 Les restrictions qu'ils se sont imposé sont à faire peur.
The restrictions which they imposed upon themselves are terrifying.

29 - **30** **Les souvenirs qu'elle s'est rappelé l'ont beaucoup ému.**
The memories which she recalled touched her deeply.

See for further information
Hawkins and Towell, 9.2–9.4
Jubb and Rouxeville, Chapters 2, 19
Judge and Healey, Chapter 8, §2.3
Byrne and Churchill, §§459–71
Ferrar, §§38–43

*Pronominal verbs are used quite frequently in French, often with no particular reflexive or reciprocal meaning. You have already seen (Day 11, Section I) that in compound tenses they take the auxiliary **être** and yesterday (Day 13, Section III) you looked at the question of past participle agreement with relation to these verbs. Today you will be focusing on other questions of usage: when and why you need to use a pronominal verb and the appropriate choice of verb form to describe a state as opposed to an action. In a couple of days' time (Day 16, Section II) you will look at a further question of usage – how a pronominal verb may be used to express a passive idea.*

I Agreement of reflexive pronoun with the subject

First, you should be careful to avoid the very common mistake of failing to make the reflexive pronoun agree with the subject. It is all too easy to use **se** regardless of the subject, and you are all the more likely to do this if you have found an unfamiliar verb in the dictionary, listed of course in the infinitive form, e.g. **s'évanouir** (to faint). The appropriate pronouns to use are as follows:

---

s'évanouir to faint

je *m'*évanouis	nous *nous* évanouissons
tu *t'*évanouis	vous *vous* évanouissez
il *s'*évanouit	ils *s'*évanouissent

Note also the present-tense forms of this regular **-ir** verb (see Day 3, Section III).

Complete the following sentences, using the pronominal verbs indicated, paying particular attention to your choice of reflexive pronoun.

---

1 Tu devrais _ _ _ _ _ _ _ _ _ _ _ _ _ _ _ _ _ _ (se reposer).
You ought to have a rest.

2 Je _ _ _ _ _ _ _ _ _ _ _ _ _ (s'occuper) de vous tout de suite. (Note: use the present tense)
I'll be with you in a minute.

3 Nous _ _ _ _ _ _ _ _ _ _ _ _ (se passer) d'elle.
We'll do without her.

---

4 Est-ce que vous _ _ _ _ _ _ _ _ _ _ _ _ (se souvenir) de lui?
Do you remember him?

5 Ils _ _ _ _ _ _ _ _ _ _ _ _ _ _ _ (se garder) de révéler le résultat.
They were careful not to give away the result.

II   Lexicalized pronominal verbs

Lexicalized pronominal verbs are simply verbs which are pronominal in form, but have no particular reflexive or reciprocal meaning. They are all intransitive, i.e. cannot take a direct object. There are two separate groups of these verbs:

* verbs which are only ever used in the pronominal form, e.g. **s'écrier** [to exclaim] and **s'évanouir** [to faint]
* verbs which have two separate entries in the dictionary – one for the simple (non-pronominal) form and one for the pronominal form. The pronominal form is lexicalized, and has a completely different meaning from the non-pronominal form.

s'en aller to go away	**s'occuper de** to look after
se décider à to make up one's mind	**se passer** to happen
se douter de to suspect	**se passer de** to do without
se moquer de to make fun of	**se rendre à** to go to

You will find a fuller listing of these verbs in Hawkins and Towell (8.7.3).

Complete the following sentences, using an appropriate pronominal verb from the list above.

6 Je dois _ _ _ _ _ _ _ _ _ _ _ _ _ _ des enfants cet après-midi.
I have to look after the children this afternoon.

7 Nous aurions dû _ _ _ _ _ _ _ _ _ _ _ _ qu'il y aurait un problème.
We should have known (suspected) that there would be a problem.

8 Elle _ _ _ _ _ _ _ _ _ _ _ _ _ _ _ à Londres en avion.
She flew to London. (= went to London by plane)

9 Vous _ _ _ _ _ _ _ _ _ _ _ de moi.
You are making fun of me.

10 Je ne peux pas _ _ _ _ _ _ _ _ _ _ _ _ _ _ _ _ de mon dictionnaire.
I can't do without my dictionary.

III   To translate an intransitive verb

In other cases, the distinction between the pronominal form of a verb and the non-pronominal form is primarily grammatical. So, for example, the pronominal form, **s'arrêter**, is intransitive (does not have a direct object), whilst the non-pronominal form, **arrêter**, is transitive (does have a direct object). Study the following examples.

La musique s'est arrêtée. The music stopped. (literally stopped itself) **J'ai arrêté le moteur.** I turned off the engine.	**Je me suis tournée vers lui.** I turned towards him. **J'ai tourné la page.** I turned the page.

There are a good number of verbs which follow this pattern, e.g. **se concentrer/concentrer** [to concentrate], **se poser** [to arise]**/poser** [to pose (a problem)], **se séparer/séparer** [to separate]. If in doubt, it is always worth checking in the dictionary to see if a verb belongs to this category.

Complete the following sentences, choosing between the pronominal and non-pronominal form of the verb.

11 **En Autriche et en Suisse les camions doivent arrêter/s'arrêter à la frontière.**
In Austria and Switzerland lorries must stop at the border.

12 **Mes pensées ont tourné/se sont tournées vers ma famille.**
My thoughts turned to my family.

13 **J'ai tourné/je me suis tourné les yeux vers lui.**
I looked at him.

14 **Je n'arrive pas à concentrer/me concentrer.**
I can't concentrate.

15 **Nous avons séparé/nous nous sommes séparés à la gare.**
We parted at the station.

There is one important special case to note. The verb **sentir** has two basic meanings: 'to feel' and 'to smell'. If you want to translate the intransitive 'to feel' + adjective/adverb, you must use the pronominal form. For example:

> **Je me sens mieux.**
> [I feel better.]
> **Elle se sent fatiguée.**
> [She feels tired.]

But what is confusing with this verb is that you do sometimes find the non-pronominal form followed by an adjective, but be warned! In this case it means 'to smell', not 'to feel'. For example:

Vous sentez bon!
[You smell nice!]

Complete the following sentences, deciding in each case whether to use **sentir** or **se sentir**.

---

16 **Elle** _ _ _ _ _ _ _ _ _ _ _ _ _ _ _ _ _ _ _ **libre de partir quand elle veut.**
She feels free to leave whenever she wants.

17 **Vous ne trouvez pas que ça** _ _ _ _ _ _ _ _ _ **mauvais?**
Don't you think it smells bad?

18 **Ils** _ _ _ _ _ _ _ _ _ _ _ _ _ _ _ **bien mieux maintenant.**
They feel a lot better now.

19 **Est-ce que vous** _ _ _ _ _ _ _ _ _ _ _ _ _ **nerveux?**
Do you feel nervous?

IV   State vs action

Many students have difficulty translating a phrase such as 'he is/was sitting'. This is a description of state, and is translated by the present/imperfect tense of **être** or **rester** followed by the past participle, **assis**. Note that you do not need a reflexive pronoun here at all. In effect, French is saying 'he is/was seated'. Avoid the common mistake of using the imperfect tense of the pronominal verb **s'asseoir**. It is important to note that **il s'asseyait** expresses an action ('he was in the process of sitting down'), not a state. There are a number of verbs relating to attitude or position which behave in the same way.

s'agenouiller to kneel	**se blottir** to nestle, snuggle, curl up
s'allonger to lie down	**se coucher** to lie down
s'appuyer to lean	**s'étendre** to lie down

Complete the following sentences, distinguishing carefully between an action and a state.

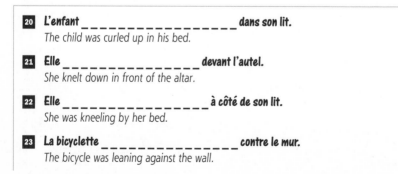

20 **L'enfant** _ _ _ _ _ _ _ _ _ _ _ _ _ _ _ _ _ _ _ **dans son lit.**
The child was curled up in his bed.

21 **Elle** _ _ _ _ _ _ _ _ _ _ _ _ _ _ _ _ _ **devant l'autel.**
She knelt down in front of the altar.

22 **Elle** _ _ _ _ _ _ _ _ _ _ _ _ _ _ _ _ _ _ **à côté de son lit.**
She was kneeling by her bed.

23 **La bicyclette** _ _ _ _ _ _ _ _ _ _ _ _ _ _ _ _ **contre le mur.**
The bicycle was leaning against the wall.

24 Elle _ _ _ _ _ _ _ _ _ _ _ _ _ _ _ _ à côté de lui.
She was sitting at his side.

25 Elle _ _ _ _ _ _ _ _ _ _ _ _ _ _ _ _ _ sur le dos.
She was lying on her back.

V General review

Look over all the points that you have covered in today's work and then correct the errors in the following sentences written by students.

26 Nous devons se rendre compte de l'importance de cette décision.
We must realize the importance of this decision.

27 Je vais concentrer sur cet aspect du problème.
I am going to concentrate on this aspect of the problem.

28 La résurgence du nationalisme se pose un grand problème.
The resurgence of nationalism poses a great problem.

29 Un enfant doit sentir en sécurité.
A child must feel safe.

30 Quand nous sommes arrivés elle s'asseyait à lire.
When we arrived she was sitting reading.

See for further information
Hawkins and Towell, 8.7
Jubb and Rouxeville, Chapter 18
Judge and Healey, Chapter 9, §2
Byrne and Churchill, §§379–81
Ferrar, §§6, 60

Key points:
The passive

DAY
15

I   Agreement of past participle
Do you sometimes forget when using the passive in French to make
the past participle agree as it should with the subject? For example:

> **Ces consignes ne sont pas respectées.**
> [These instructions are not respected.]
> **Ma voiture a été réparée hier.**
> [My car was repaired yesterday.]
> **Ils ont été licenciés.**
> [They have been made redundant.]

Always check your work carefully for this point.

Look again at the second and third examples above and note that it is the past
participle of the main verbs that agree (**réparée**, **licenciés**), not the past participle
of the auxiliary (**été**).

Correct the errors in the following sentences written by students.

1   **Nos grands-parents n'ont pas été exposé à ces dangers.**
   Our grandparents were not exposed to these dangers.

2   **Plusieurs de ses romans ont étés adapté pour le cinéma.**
   Several of his novels have been adapted for the cinema.

3   **Sans l'aide de la communauté internationale, certaines minorités ethniques
   risquent d'être complètement anéanti.**
   Without the help of the international community, some ethnic minorities are in
   danger of being completely wiped out.

4   **Cette pièce a été crée à la Comédie Française.**
   This play was put on for the first time at the Comédie Française.

II   Formation problems
Remember that the passive is formed by using the appropriate form of **être** + a
past participle and watch out for the following common errors.

Never be tempted to use an infinitive instead of a past participle. For example:

> **La langue française serait trop anglicisée**. (not **angliciser**)
> [The French language is supposedly too anglicized.]

Make sure you can conjugate **être** in all its moods and tenses. Remember that in the compound tenses, it takes the auxiliary **avoir** (see Day 11). For example:

> **La voiture aura été réparée.**
> [The car will have been repaired.]
> **La voiture aurait été réparée.**
> [The car would have been repaired.]
> **La voiture avait été réparée.**
> [The car had been repaired.]
> **Je regrette que la voiture n'ait pas été réparée.**
> [I'm sorry that the car has not been repaired.]

Rewrite the following sentences in the passive. For example:

> **Ma copine a écrit cet article. > Cet article a été écrit par ma copine.**
> [My friend has written this article. > This article has been written by my friend.]

Don't forget past participle agreements where necessary!

---

5 **Mon chef paie mes frais de déplacement.**
My boss pays my travel expenses.

6 **Leur mère n'aurait jamais abandonné ces enfants.**
Their mother would never have abandoned these children.

7 **Cette crise a désuni la famille.**
This crisis has broken up the family.

8 **La jeune fille au pair gardera les enfants.**
The au pair girl will look after the children.

9 **Les étudiants avaient organisé des élections.**
The students had organized elections.

10 **Que le spectacle désarme les critiques!**
May the show disarm the critics!

Be very careful with the passive infinitive, which is formed from the infinitive **être** + a past participle. For example:

> **Ils vont être exposés** (not **exposer**) **à des dangers considérables.**
> [They will be exposed to considerable dangers.]

Rewrite the following sentences in the passive.

11 **Cette aventure risque d'épuiser l'équipe.**
This adventure may well exhaust the team.

12 **Ce fait pourrait expliquer son absence.**
This fact might explain his absence.

III Choice of past tense

Do you sometimes automatically use the imperfect of **être** to translate a passive construction with 'was/were'? Many students do, but this is not appropriate when a completed event is involved. Instead, you should use the past historic (or alternatively the passé composé). For example:

L'Académie française fut fondée en 1635 par Richelieu.
[The French Academy was founded in 1635 by Richelieu.]

If in doubt about whether to use the imperfect or the past historic/passé composé, try the sentence out first in the active and follow the same tense usage in the passive. For example:

Richelieu fonda l'Académie française en 1635.
[Richelieu founded the French Academy in 1635.]

Remember that the imperfect is only appropriate for the following:

• Ongoing actions/states, where the imperfect would also be used in the active sentence. For example:

Tous le respectaient.
[Everyone respected him.]
Il était respecté de tous.
[He was respected by everyone.]

Note that when an ongoing state is involved, the agent is usually introduced by **de** rather than **par**.

• Repeated/habitual actions, where again the imperfect would be used in the active sentence. For example:

On ouvrait la porte tous les jours à huit heures.
[They opened the gate every day at eight o'clock.]
La porte était ouverte tous les jours à huit heures.
[The gate was opened every day at eight o'clock.]

Complete the following sentences, paying particular attention to the choice of past tense.

---

13   **Ce bâtiment** _ _ _ _ _ _ _ _ _ _ _ _ _ _ _ _ **par un architecte célèbre.**
This building was designed by a famous architect. (**concevoir** – *to design*)

14   **Nous** _ _ _ _ _ _ _ _ _ _ _ _ _ _ _ _ _ _ _ **à dîner hier par nos nouveaux voisins.**
We were invited to dinner yesterday by our new neighbours.

15   **Elle** _ _ _ _ _ _ _ _ _ _ _ _ _ _ **d'entendre qu'il avait réussi à son examen.**
She was amazed to hear that he had passed his exam.

16   **Le rédacteur** _ _ _ _ _ _ _ _ _ _ _ _ _ _ _ _ **de ses collègues.**
The editor was very well thought of by his colleagues. (**bien voir** – *to think well of*)

IV   Cases where the passive cannot be used

Problems often arise when students try to turn the indirect object of an active sentence into the subject of a passive. In French it is only possible to turn the direct object of an active sentence into the subject of a passive. For example:

> Active: **Le réalisateur a donné le rôle de Cathy à Juliette Binoche.**
> [The director gave the role of Cathy to Juliette Binoche.]
> Passive: **Le rôle de Cathy a été donné à Juliette Binoche.**
> [The role of Cathy was given to Juliette Binoche.]
> ***Juliette Binoche a été donné le rôle de Cathy.** *Impossible construction*

In other words, the English sentence, 'Juliette Binoche was given the role of Cathy' cannot be directly translated into French. There are a number of French verbs which pose this problem and it is important for you to be able to identify them and their indirect objects. You need to watch out for:

- verbs like **donner** which take the construction (**donner**) **quelque chose à quelqu'un**;
- verbs like **demander** which take the construction (**demander**) **à quelqu'un de faire quelque chose**.
- verbs introducing reported speech, e.g. **dire à quelqu'un que . . .**

It may sometimes help to twist the English sentence around. For example:

> He gave me a present. > He gave a present **to me** (indirect object).

But the only way to be really sure is to know the construction used with the French verb.

Read the following sentences and without translating them, indicate which of them you could translate directly into French with a passive (Yes) and which would require a different approach (No).

17 *His assistant was offered a new job.*

18 *She was forced to complete the course.*

19 *They were sold a faulty machine.*

20 *He was taught to play bridge at school.*

Look again at number 17. It is impossible to translate this directly into French, because 'his assistant' would have been the indirect object of the active sentence, 'Someone offered a new job to his assistant'. Instead, you could either take the direct object of the active sentence and make it the subject of a passive construction:

Un nouveau poste a été offert à son assistant.

[A new job was offered to his assistant.]

Or you could use **on** with an active verb:

On a offert un nouveau poste à son assistant.

[They offered a new job/A new job was offered to his assistant.]

Complete the following sentences using **on** with an active verb.

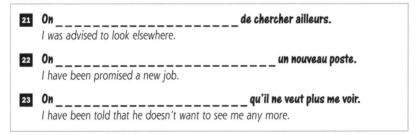

21 *On _____ de chercher ailleurs.*
I was advised to look elsewhere.

22 *On _____ un nouveau poste.*
I have been promised a new job.

23 *On _____ qu'il ne veut plus me voir.*
I have been told that he doesn't want to see me any more.

V Se voir, s'entendre + infinitive

An alternative way of translating sentences 21–3 is to use **se voir** followed by an infinitive. For example:

Je me suis vu promettre un nouveau poste.

[I have been promised (literally, 'I have seen myself promised') a new job.]

When a verb of saying/telling is involved, it is more usual to find **s'entendre** + infinitive. For example:

Je me suis entendu dire qu'il ne veut plus me voir.
[I have been told (literally, 'I have heard myself being told') that he no longer wants to see me.]

This construction is particularly useful in cases where it is impossible to use **on**, because a specific agent is mentioned. For example:

Je me suis entendu dire <u>par un collègue</u> que le PDG allait démissionner.
I was told <u>by a colleague </u>that the managing director was going to resign.

 There is one great danger to watch with this construction. You must remember that, unlike the true passive (see Section II above), it is followed by an infinitive and not by a past participle.

Complete the following sentences using **se voir** or **s'entendre** + infinitive. Note: Although you will find that usage varies in this respect, it is advisable not to make an agreement between the past participle and the preceding pronoun with **se voir**, **s'entendre**. For example:

Elle s'est vu décerner le premier prix.
[She was awarded the first prize.]
Ils se sont entendu dire le résultat.
[They were told the result.]

---

24 **Nous _ _ _ _ _ _ _ _ _ _ _ _ _ _ _ _ un nouvel appartement par le propriétaire.**
We have been offered a new flat by the landlord.

25 **Nous _ l'accès du bâtiment.**
We have been denied admittance to the building. (Use **refuser***)*

26 **Elle _ _ _ _ _ _ _ _ _ _ _ _ _ _ _ de partir dès que possible.**
She was advised to leave as soon as possible.

Correct the error in the following sentence written by a student.

---

27 **Tout cela se passe dans un pays qui s'est vu divisé en deux états après la deuxième guerre mondiale.**
All this is happening in a country which was divided into two states after the Second World War.

Finally, rewrite the following sentences, replacing the ungrammatical passive constructions with a suitable alternative.

28 **Ils ont été donné le choix de rester en Algérie ou de retourner en France.**
They were given the choice of staying in Algeria or returning to France.

29 **Il a été demandé de payer en avance.**
He was asked to pay in advance.

30 **J'ai été montré le nouveau bâtiment.**
I was shown the new building.

You will no doubt have met a number of other alternatives to the passive in French and the next section, Day 16, gives you the opportunity to revise and practise these.

See for further information
Hawkins and Towell, 8.8.6
Jubb and Rouxeville, Chapter 19
Judge and Healey, Chapter 9, §3, Chapter 10, §6
Byrne and Churchill, §§382–5
Ferrar, §§5, 61

I   Use an active verb

You saw in Day 15 how **on** + an active verb is a useful alternative when a passive construction is grammatically impossible. It is also used more widely, even when a passive would be grammatically possible. For example:

> **On a arrêté les cambrioleurs.** (as an alternative to: **Les cambrioleurs ont été arrêtés.**)
> [The burglars have been arrested.]

However, remember that you cannot use **on** in the following cases:

* when the action is not performed by a human being. For example:

La ville a été inondée.
[The town was flooded.]

* when the agent, human or non-human, is specified:

La lettre a été tapée par la secrétaire.
[The letter was typed by the secretary.]
L'arbre a été touché par la foudre.
[The tree was struck by lightning.]

Without translating the following, indicate which sentences could be translated into French using **on** + active verb (Yes) and which could not (No).

> **1**   I had the sun in my eyes and was momentarily blinded.
>
> **2**   He is said to be dangerously ill.
>
> **3**   He was seen leaving at midnight.
>
> **4**   The house was struck by lightning.

When the agent is specified, and it is therefore not possible to use **on** + active verb, a good option is to turn the sentence round into an active sentence. For example:

> **Le directeur lui a demandé de partir.**
> [She was asked by the director to leave.]

Translate the following into French, turning the sentences round and using an active verb in each case.

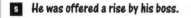

> **5** **He was offered a rise by his boss.**
>
> **6** **She was taught to drive by her father.**

II Use a pronominal verb
You can also use a pronominal verb to translate an English passive. For example:

> **Cela ne se fait pas.**
> [That is not done.]

Rewrite the following sentences, using a reflexive verb.

> **7** **On boit le champagne frais.**
> *Champagne is drunk chilled.*
>
> **8** **On vendait les fraises à trente francs le kilo.**
> *Strawberries were being sold at thirty francs a kilo.*
>
> **9** **Le centre-ville a été transformé.**
> *The town centre has been transformed.*
>
> **10** **Enfin la porte fut ouverte.**
> *At last the door was opened.*

But it is not possible to use this construction with all verbs, and it is always impossible if the agent is expressed. So you cannot say

> ***Cela se fait par de nombreux gens.**
> [That is done by many people.]

It is also impossible if the subject is a person. For example:

> **Ils ont été arrêtés.**
> [They were arrested.]

The use of a pronominal verb here, **Ils se sont arrêtés** ['They stopped'], would mean something completely different.

Without translating the following, indicate which sentences could be translated into French using a pronominal verb (Yes) and which could not (No).

> **11** **The historical centre of the town can be visited on foot.**
>
> **12** **This wine is not drunk by the locals.**
>
> **13** **She was wrongfully imprisoned.**
>
> **14** **This is a bird which is very rarely seen in Britain.**

III Use *se faire, se laisser* + infinitive

Se faire + infinitive translates 'to get oneself' + English past participle. For example:

> ### Elle s'est fait arrêter.
> [She was/got herself arrested.]

Se laisser + infinitive translates 'to let oneself be' + English past participle. For example:

> ### Ils se sont laissé avoir.
> [They were/let themselves be conned.]

In both cases, there is the idea that the subject somehow contributed to what happened, or at least allowed it to happen. Note that as with **se voir**, **s'entendre** + infinitive (see Day 15, Section V), there is usually no agreement between the past participle and the preceding pronoun.

 Rewrite the following sentences, using **se faire** or **se laisser** + infinitive. Remember always to use an infinitive after these verbs, and not the past participle which occurs in the original passive construction.

> **15** **Il a été harcelé par les manifestants.**
> *He was harassed by the demonstrators.*
>
> **16** **Elle a été trompée par son mari.**
> *She was cheated on by her husband.*
>
> **17** **Si tu ne fais pas attention, tu vas être piqué.**
> *If you're not careful, you'll get stung.*

IV   Use *se voir, s'entendre* + infinitive

Look back to Day 15, Section V, and revise the use of **se voir/s'entendre** + infinitive to translate an English passive. There you practised using them with verbs like **donner** where a literal translation with a French passive would not be possible. They can also be used with verbs where it would be possible to use a true passive in French. For example:

> **Il s'est vu élire président du conseil.**
> [He was elected chairman of the council.]
> **Il a été élu président du conseil.**
> [He was elected chairman of the council.]

Again, as with **se faire**, **se laisser**, always remember to use an infinitive after **se voir, s'entendre**.

Rewrite the following sentences, using **se voir** or **s'entendre** + infinitive.

---

18   **Il a été nommé à Aix.**
He was posted to Aix.

19   **Elle a été promue du rang de secrétaire.**
She was promoted from the rank of secretary.

20   **L'équipe sera reléguée dans la division inférieure.**
The team will be relegated to the lower division.

V   Use an abstract noun

You can sometimes avoid a verbal construction altogether in French by using an abstract noun. For example:

> **Nous avons vu la démolition de l'immeuble.**
> [We saw the block of flats being pulled down.]

Translate the following sentences into French, using an abstract noun to translate the English passive construction.

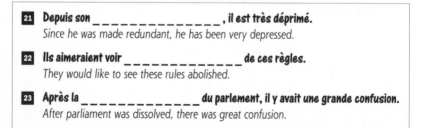

21   **Depuis son _ _ _ _ _ _ _ _ _ _ _ _ _ _ , il est très déprimé.**
Since he was made redundant, he has been very depressed.

22   **Ils aimeraient voir _ _ _ _ _ _ _ _ _ _ _ _ _ de ces règles.**
They would like to see these rules abolished.

23   **Après la _ _ _ _ _ _ _ _ _ _ _ _ du parlement, il y avait une grande confusion.**
After parliament was dissolved, there was great confusion.

VI Use *être à*

This is very useful for translating a modal verb, e.g. should, must + passive. For example:

> **C'est une occasion à ne pas manquer.**
> [This is an opportunity not to be missed.]
> **Cette lettre est à retaper.**
> [This letter must be retyped.]
> **Ils sont à plaindre.**
> [They are to be pitied.]

Complete the following sentences, using **être à** + infinitive.

---

24 *Ce rapport* _____ *aujourd'hui.*
This report must be completed today.

25 *Son devoir* _____ *entièrement* _____.
His paper had to be completely rewritten.

26 *Ces papiers* _____.
These papers are to be thrown out.

VII General review

Finally, test yourself on all that you have learnt in this unit by finding suitable alternatives to the passive when you complete the following sentences.

---

27 *Elle* _____ *tant bien que mal.*
She made herself understood with great difficulty.

28 *Ce n'est pas une femme avec qui* _____ !
(to trifle with – badiner avec)
She is not someone to be trifled with!

29 *Cela* _____ *jamais.*
That is never written.

30 *Nous attendons* _____ *des marchandises.*
We are waiting for the goods to be delivered.

See for further information

Hawkins and Towell, 8.7.4, 8.7.6
Jubb and Rouxeville, Chapter 19
Judge and Healey, Chapter 9, §§2.3, 2.4
Byrne and Churchill, §§384–5
Ferrar, §61

I Third-person subject pronouns: *il(s)*, *elle(s)*

Remember that the pronouns **il(s)** and **elle(s)** are used to refer to inanimates as well as to people and animals. Be careful to check the gender of your nouns and always use **elle(s)** to refer to a feminine noun. Don't fall into the trap of thinking in English and translating 'it'/ 'they' as **il(s)** regardless. This is another place to watch for agreements. For example:

Cette remarque vous semble-t-*elle* juste?
[Does this remark seem valid to you?]
Les élections ont été reportées. *Elles* auront lieu la semaine prochaine.
[The elections have been postponed. They will take place next week.]

If your subject consists of a feminine noun or nouns together with one or more masculines, then the pronoun will be masculine plural. For example:

Est-ce que tu as vu les azalées (fpl) **et les rhododendrons** (mpl)? ***Ils* sont vraiment magnifiques.**
[Have you seen the azaleas and rhododendrons? They are really magnificent.]

Complete the sentences below with the appropriate subject pronoun.

1 **La lettre a été expédiée hier. _ _ _ _ _ aurait dû arriver au siège de l'entreprise ce matin.**
The letter was sent off yesterday. It should have reached the head office this morning.

2 **Ces personnes ont été interrogées par la police. _ _ _ _ _ ne savent pas pourquoi.**
These people were questioned by the police. They don't know why.

3 **Je ne trouve pas mes clefs, mais _ _ _ _ _ _ étaient sur mon bureau tout à l'heure, j'en suis sûr.**
I can't find my keys, but they were on my desk a little while ago, I'm sure.

4 *Ces groupes vont se réunir à la fin. _ _ _ _ ont l'intention d'organiser une sortie ensemble.*
These groups are going to meet up at the end. They intend to organize an outing together.

5 *Vous allez voir d'abord le château et la chapelle. _ _ _ _ _ datent du quatorzième siècle.*
You will see the castle and the chapel first of all. They date from the fourteenth century.

II   Direct/indirect object pronouns

No problem in the first and second persons where the forms (**me**, **te**, **nous, vous**) are the same for direct and indirect objects. The problem arises in the third person, where you have to choose between the direct object pronouns (**le**, **la**, **l'**, **les**) and the indirect (**lui**, **leur**). Two things to watch for here.

First, and most important, always make sure you know the construction of the verb in French. If it takes **à** + person (indirect object), then you need an indirect object pronoun. For example:

> **Je téléphone <u>à Jean-Pierre</u>**, so **Je lui téléphone.**
> [I ring Jean-Pierre. I ring him.]
> **Il ressemble <u>à son frère</u>**, so **Il lui ressemble.**
> [He looks like his brother. He looks like him.]
> **On conseille <u>aux étudiants</u> de passer au moins trois mois en France**, so **On leur conseille . . .**
> [Students are advised to spend at least three months in France. They are advised . . .]
> **Il apprend <u>aux enfants</u> à nager**, so **Il leur apprend à nager.**
> [He is teaching the children to swim. He is teaching them to swim.]

Many of these verbs, as you will see, take a direct object in English, and that is the danger.

Second, make sure that the French verb really does take **à** + person (indirect object). Confusion sometimes arises with verbs which in fact take a direct object, but which require **à** before a following infinitive. The most common error is with **aider**. For example:

> **J'aide mes parents à déménager. Je les aide à déménager**.
> [I am helping my parents to move house. I am helping them to move house.]

Rewrite the following sentences, replacing the underlined words with the appropriate pronouns.

---

6 **On offre des places gratuites aux étudiants.**
Free places are offered to students.

7 **Ce cadeau a beaucoup plu à mon père.**
My father liked this present a lot.

8 **Ses parents ont encouragé Jean-Luc à chercher un travail à l'étranger.**
His parents encouraged Jean-Luc to find a job abroad.

9 **Ce travail a donné beaucoup de soucis aux éditeurs.**
This work caused the publishers a lot of problems.

How would you fill the gaps in the following sentences, in each case translating English 'them'?

---

10 **Ils ont demandé à leurs parents de _ _ _ _ acheter des baskets.**
They have asked their parents to buy them some trainers.

11 **Les enfants ont compris que leurs parents pouvaient _ _ _ _ aider à faire leurs devoirs.**
The children realized that their parents could help them to do their homework.

12 **Ce qui _ _ _ _ ennuie, c'est le manque de temps libre.**
What bothers them is the lack of free time.

Finally, check your answers and make sure you have not put an **-s** on any of your uses of **leur**. You will only ever find **leurs** with an **-s** when it is either a possessive adjective, e.g. **leurs parents** [their parents] in sentences 10 and 11 above, or a possessive pronoun, e.g. **Ils ont jeté mes cartes, mais j'ai gardé les leurs**. [They threw away my cards, but I kept theirs.]

Fill in the gaps in the following sentence with either **leur** or **leurs** as appropriate.

---

13 - 14 **Il _ _ _ _ _ a téléphoné des Etats-Unis pour avoir de _ _ _ _ _ nouvelles.**
He rang from the States to ask after them.

III   Direct object pronouns preceded by *à* or *de*

Make sure that when the object pronouns **le**, **les** are preceded by the prepositions **à** or **de**, they remain unchanged. For example:

> **Elle m'a demandé de les inviter.**
> [She has asked me to invite them.]
> **Elle m'a aidé à le terminer.**
> [She helped me to finish it.]

The contracted forms **au(x)** and **du/des** represent **à/de** + definite article (see Day 7).

Rewrite the following sentences, replacing the underlined words by the appropriate pronoun.

---

15   *Avez-vous les moyens de payer ces travaux?*
Do you have the means to pay for this work?

16   *Je suis arrivé à configurer mon ordinateur.*
I have managed to set up my computer.

17   *Il a persuadé ses parents de payer son voyage.*
He persuaded his parents to pay for his trip.

18   *Je vais aider ma soeur à déballer ses affaires.*
I'm going to help my sister to unpack her things.

IV   Use of *en*

Two things to focus on here. First, you often need to use **en** where there would be no equivalent at all in English. For example:

> **Combien de ses films avez-vous vus? J'en ai vu quatre.**
> [How many of his films have you seen? I've seen four.]

Second, watch out for verbs which take **de**, e.g. **avoir besoin de**, **avoir envie de**, **douter de**, **se passer de**, **se servir de**. You must not use the direct object pronouns **le**, **la**, **l'**, **les** with these verbs. Use **en** instead. It replaces **de** + noun/pronoun or **de** + infinitive. For example:

> **Nous avons besoin de ces documents. Nous en avons besoin.**
> [We need these documents. We need them.]
> **Je me sers de son portable. Je m'en sers.**
> [I'm using her/his laptop. I'm using it.]
> **J'ai envie de partir. J'en ai envie.**
> [I want to leave. I want to (do so).]

Don't be misled by English in cases like the first two, where we would use a direct object pronoun.

Complete the following sentences, using **en** where appropriate.

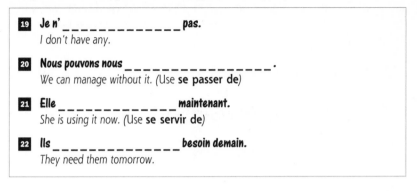

19 Je n' _ _ _ _ _ _ _ _ _ _ _ _ _ pas.
I don't have any.

20 Nous pouvons nous _ _ _ _ _ _ _ _ _ _ _ _ _ _ _ _ _.
We can manage without it. (Use **se passer de**)

21 Elle _ _ _ _ _ _ _ _ _ _ _ _ maintenant.
She is using it now. (Use **se servir de**)

22 Ils _ _ _ _ _ _ _ _ _ _ _ _ _ besoin demain.
They need them tomorrow.

V Use of y

The main thing to avoid here is confusion with **en**. Whereas **en** replaces **de** + noun/pronoun, or **de** + infinitive, **y** replaces **à**, **dans, en, sur** + noun, or **à** + infinitive. For example:

Je tiens beaucoup à mon appartement. J'y tiens beaucoup.
[I'm very fond of my flat. I'm very fond of it.]

The classic problem case arises with **penser à** (to think, reflect about) and **penser de** (to have an opinion about). Compare the following:

Je pense à partir. Je pense aux examens.
[I'm thinking about leaving. I'm thinking about the exams.]

Both become **J'y pense**. [I'm thinking about it/them.]

Que pensez-vous de ce nouveau bâtiment?
[What do you think of this new building?]

This becomes **Qu'en pensez-vous?** [What do you think of it?]

First, correct the pronoun error in the following sentence written by a student.

23 Il y a autant de gens qui veulent contester les normes répandues que de personnes qui préfèrent s'en adhérer.
There are as many people who want to challenge generally accepted norms as who prefer to subscribe to them. (Note the construction: **s'adhérer à quelque chose**.)

Now rewrite the following sentences, replacing the underlined words by either **y** or **en** as appropriate. Hint: Note in each case the preposition (**à**, **de**, **sur**) with which the underlined phrase begins. Don't be put off by any other prepositions which occur later in the phrase.

24 Elle a signé son nom <u>sur la page de titre.</u>
She signed her name on the title page.

25 Est-ce que tu as pensé <u>à l'anniversaire de ton oncle?</u>
Have you remembered your uncle's birthday?

26 Je ne sais pas ce que vous pensez <u>de cela.</u>
I don't know what you think of that?

27 Je te demande de faire très attention <u>aux livres de ton père.</u>
Please be very careful with your father's books.

28 Je suis allé <u>au Musée de l'Homme à Paris.</u>
I went to the Musée de l'Homme in Paris.

29 Je n'ai aucune envie d'aller <u>à la plage.</u>
I have no wish to go to the beach.

30 Si vous pouviez être des nôtres, nous serions ravis <u>de vous voir.</u>
If you could join us, we would be delighted to see you.

See for further information
Hawkins and Towell, Chapter 3
Jubb and Rouxeville, Chapter 10
Judge and Healey, Chapter 3, §1
Byrne and Churchill, §§193–20
Ferrar, §§154–67

I   Use of *ne*
Do you sometimes forget to use **ne** before the verb in negative constructions? It is true that **ne** frequently is omitted in less formal varieties of French, particularly in speech, but you should avoid the mistake of omitting it in formal written French. Watch out particularly with the following:

personne, rien, aucun(e), ni . . . ni as subject, e.g. **Personne *ne* le comprend**. No-one understands it/him. **Rien *ne* l'intéresse.** Nothing interests her/him.	**Aucun problème *ne* se présentera.** No problem will arise. **Ni lui ni sa sœur *ne* pourront nous rejoindre.** Neither he nor his sister will be able to join us.

If the sentence begins with **jamais**, you still need **ne** before the verb. For example:

> **Jamais je ne lui dirai la vérité.**
> [Never will I tell her/him the truth.]

You also need **ne** when **jamais, personne, rien, aucun, ni . . . ni** follow the verb, but that tends to be easier to remember. For example:

> **Je n'ai vu personne.**
> [I haven't seen anyone.]
> **Il ne comprend rien.**
> [He doesn't understand anything.]
> **Il n'a aucun talent.**
> [He has no talent.]
> **Je n'ai ni le temps ni l'argent pour cela.**
> [I have neither the time nor the money for that.]

Complete the following sentences, remembering always to use **ne** before the verb.

1   Rien _ _ _ _ _ _ _ _changer.
Nothing is going to change.

2   Personne _ _ _ _ _ _ _ _ _ _ce qui se passe.
No-one knows what is happening.

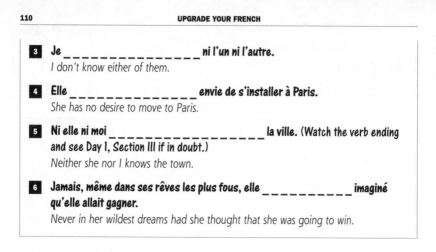

3 Je _ _ _ _ _ _ _ _ _ _ _ _ _ ni l'un ni l'autre.
I don't know either of them.

4 Elle _ _ _ _ _ _ _ _ _ _ _ _ _ envie de s'installer à Paris.
She has no desire to move to Paris.

5 Ni elle ni moi _ _ _ _ _ _ _ _ _ _ _ _ _ _ _ la ville. (Watch the verb ending and see Day I, Section III if in doubt.)
Neither she nor I knows the town.

6 Jamais, même dans ses rêves les plus fous, elle _ _ _ _ _ _ _ _ _ imaginé qu'elle allait gagner.
Never in her wildest dreams had she thought that she was going to win.

II   Misuse of *pas*

Students sometimes make the mistake of using **pas** in conjunction with **ne . . . jamais**, **ne . . . personne**, **ne . . . rien**, etc. Make sure that you avoid this mistake. It is possible, however, to combine other negative particles. For example:

> **Il ne fait plus rien.**
> [He doesn't do anything any more.]
> **Elle ne s'achète jamais rien.**
> [She never buys anything for herself.]

Rewrite the following sentences to express the meaning indicated by the English in brackets.

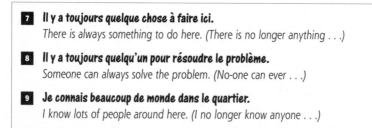

7 Il y a toujours quelque chose à faire ici.
There is always something to do here. (There is no longer anything . . .)

8 Il y a toujours quelqu'un pour résoudre le problème.
Someone can always solve the problem. (No-one can ever . . .)

9 Je connais beaucoup de monde dans le quartier.
I know lots of people around here. (I no longer know anyone . . .)

III   Word order

Do you have problems knowing where to place the negative particles with verbs in compound tenses? Remember the following:

- **ne** always precedes both the verb and any object pronouns. For example:

> **Je ne l'ai pas fait.**
> [I didn't do it.]
> **Ne l'avez-vous pas vu?**
> [Haven't you seen it?]

Vous ne vous êtes pas trompé.
[You have not made a mistake.]

- Group 1 expressions: **pas**, **point**, **plus**, **guère**, **jamais**, **rien** come after the auxiliary verb and before the past participle. For example:

Je ne l'ai jamais vu.
[I have never seen it.]
N'avez-vous pas fini?
[Haven't you finished?]
Il n'est plus retourné en France.
[He hasn't been back to France again.]

- Group 2 expressions: **personne**, **que**, **aucun**, **nul**, **nulle part**, **ni . . . ni** all follow the past participle. For example:

Il n'a vu personne.
[He hasn't seen anyone.]
Nous n'avons vu que les épreuves de tournage.
[We have only seen the rushes.]
Ils n'ont fait aucun effort.
[They haven't made any effort.]

Rewrite the following sentences, replacing the underlined word(s) with a negative.

---

10 **Avez-vous vu quelque chose?**
  Have you seen something? (Haven't you seen anything?)

11 **Elle l'a toujours aimé.**
  She has always loved him. (She has never loved him.)

12 **Avez-vous vu quelqu'un?**
  Have you seen someone? (Haven't you seen anyone?)

13 **On en a trouvé partout.**
  We found them everywhere. (We couldn't find any anywhere.)

14 **Elle avait étudié tous les dossiers.**
  She had examined all the files. (She hadn't examined any of the files.)

When negative particles occur with infinitives, remember the following:

- Group 1 expressions both come together in front of the infinitive. For example:

Je regrette de ne pas pouvoir y assister.
[I'm sorry I can't be there.]
Il reste pendant des heures à ne rien faire.
[He spends hours doing nothing.]

- Group 2 expressions behave as they would with a finite verb, i.e. **ne** before the verb and the second element after it. For example:

Je l'ai remercié de n'en avoir parlé à personne.
I thanked her/him for not having spoken to anyone about this.

Rewrite the following sentences, negating the underlined words and paying attention to word order.

15   **Je lui ai demandé de parler à Sandrine.**
I asked her/him to speak (not to speak) to Sandrine.

16   **Je lui ai demandé de parler à tout le monde.**
I asked her/him to speak to everyone. (not to speak to anyone.)

17   **Nous préférons dîner avant vingt heures.**
We prefer to have dinner (not to have dinner) before eight p.m.

18   **Il a envie de faire quelque chose.**
He wants to do something. (He feels like doing nothing.)

IV   *ne . . . que* ('only')

Be careful to place the **que** immediately before the word or phrase to which the idea of 'only' applies. Contrast the following:

> **Je ne m'accorde un verre de vin que le samedi soir.**
> [I allow myself a glass of wine only on Saturday evenings.]
> **Je ne m'accorde qu'un verre de vin le samedi soir.**
> [I allow myself only one glass of wine on Saturday evenings.]

Rewrite these sentences, using **ne . . . que** in order to convey the meaning indicated by the English.

19   **Une mère peut travailler si elle a l'aide et le soutien de sa famille.**
A mother can work only if she has the help and support of her family.

20   **C'est lui qui s'occupe du jardin.**
He's the only one who attends to the garden)

21   **On trouve ces plantes à basse altitude.**
You find these plants only at low altitude.

22   **On trouve ces plantes à haute altitude.**
You find only these plants at high altitude.

23   **Elle réussit ses examens après de longues heures de préparation.**
She passes her exams only after long hours of preparation.

V   Use of articles

You saw in Day 7, Section IV, that with the direct object of a negative verb, **de** is normally substituted for the partitive article, **du**, **de la**, **de l'** and for the indefinite article **un(e)**, **des**. For example:

> **Je n'ai pas de voiture.**
> [I don't have a car.]
> **Ils ne font pas de voyages.**
> [They don't do any travelling.]
> **Il ne me reste plus de sucre.**
> [I haven't any more sugar left.]

There are some warnings to make here. First, this substitution does not occur after **ne ... que** (see Day 7). For example:

> **Il ne me reste que du café.**
> [I only have coffee left.]
> **Elle ne mange que des pommes.**
> [She only eats apples.]

Definite articles remain unchanged after a negative. For example:

> **Je n'aime pas l'alcool.**
> [I don't like alcohol.]
> **Ils n'aiment pas les voyages.**
> [They don't like travelling.]

Students sometimes make the mistake of writing **pas de tout** instead of **pas du tout** [not at all]. Make sure you don't do this!

Rewrite the following sentences in the negative, making any necessary changes to the articles.

---

24 **Ils adorent les enfants.**
They love (don't love) children.

25 **Elle a fait une erreur.**
She has made a mistake. (hasn't made a mistake)

26 **Il reste des chambres simples.**
There are some basic rooms left. (There are no basic rooms left.)

IV   General review

Test yourself on the whole of this unit by correcting any mistakes which you find in the following sentences.

27   **Je n'ai acheté rien.**
I haven't bought anything.

28   **Elle ne comprend pas de tout ce qu'il raconte.**
She can't understand what he's talking about at all.

29   **Personne me l'a jamais expliqué.**
No-one has ever explained it to me.

30   **Je leur avais demandé de ne téléphoner pas après minuit.**
I had asked them not to ring after midnight.

See for further information
Hawkins and Towell, Chapter 16
Jubb and Rouxeville, Chapter 8
Judge and Healey, Chapter 12, §7
Byrne and Churchill, §§542–80
Ferrar, §§248–53

Do you avoid using inversion of verb and subject because you are not entirely confident about handling it and are unsure in any case when it is appropriate? You will notice in your reading that the placing of the subject after the verb is a frequent feature of formal written French. By making a conscious effort to use such inversion in your own writing you can make a significant improvement to your style.

I Interrogative sentences

First, a note about **est-ce que** which is a very frequently used way of asking a question without using inversion. It involves no change to the direct word order (subject, verb, complement); you simply put it at the beginning of a yes/no question. For example:

> **Est-ce que tu travailles ce soir?**
> [Are you working this evening?]

Or immediately after an initial question word. For example:

> **Comment est-ce que tu vas t'y prendre?**
> [How are you going to set about it?]

This is all very straightforward, but watch out for the common error of omitting the third-person singular verb, **est**, when it occurs in a question introduced by **est-ce que**. For example:

> **Est-ce que le thème *est* vraiment nécessaire?**
> [Is prose composition really necessary?]

Turn the following statements into questions, using **est-ce que**.

> **1** **Cet ingrédient est absolument essentiel.**
> *This ingredient is absolutely essential.*

> **2** **Ce cours est intéressant.**
> *This course is interesting.*

However, in more formal style, such as essay-writing, you should be trying to use inversion instead of **est-ce que**. There are two forms of inversion which you need to distinguish: simple inversion and complex inversion.

i)   Simple inversion
This involves placing the verb before the subject. Before deciding whether it is possible to use simple inversion in a question you must first note whether the subject is a noun or a pronoun. **With a pronoun subject**, simple inversion can always be used. For example:

> **Avez-vous vu ce film?**
> [Have you seen this film?]
> **Comment allez-vous?**
> [How are you?]

Two small things to note:

* The verb and subject pronoun are linked by a hyphen.
* After a third-person verb ending in a vowel, you must insert a **-t-** before the subject pronoun (**elle, il, on**). For example:

A-t-elle terminé son travail?
[Has she finished her work?]
Comment va-t-il s'en sortir?
[How is he going to manage?]
Quand va-t-on comprendre?
[When will they understand?]

With a noun subject, simple inversion is always used after **que**. For example:

> **Que disent les experts?**
> [What do the experts say?]
> **Que sont devenus ses parents?**
> [What has become of his parents?]

This is the formal equivalent of **Qu'est-ce que** and direct word order (subject, verb), e.g. **Qu'est-ce que les experts disent? Qu'est-ce que ses parents sont devenus?** Simple inversion may also be used in some circumstances after the question words, **combien**, **comment**, **quand**, **où**, **qui** and also after **quoi** preceded by a preposition. For example:

> **En quoi consiste mon erreur?**
> [Where have I gone wrong?]
> **Quand viendra le printemps?**
> [When will spring come?]

But there are restrictions on this usage. If in doubt, it is safer always to use complex inversion after these question words (see below).

ii) Complex inversion

This is used with a noun subject. First, you state the noun subject, followed by the verb, then you repeat the subject by placing an appropriate subject pronoun after the verb. For example:

Pourquoi cette proposition a-t-elle été refusée?
[Why has this proposal been rejected?]

With a noun subject, you must use complex inversion in formal written French in the following circumstances:

• In questions which invite a yes/no answer. For example:

La bibliothèque est-elle ouverte le soir?
[Is the library open in the evening?]

• After the question word **pourquoi**. For example:

Pourquoi le train est-il en retard?
[Why is the train late?]

• After other question words when the direct object of the verb is a noun or when the verb **être** or **devenir** is followed by a noun or adjective complement. For example:

Quand le professeur va-t-il corriger les copies?
[When is the teacher going to mark the papers?]
Quand Jacques Chirac est-il devenu président?
[When did Jacques Chirac become president?]

First correct the errors in the following questions written by students.

> **3** *Pourquoi existe-elle?*
> *Why does it exist?*
>
> **4** *Pourquoi devraient payer les contribuables britanniques une telle chose?*
> *Why should British taxpayers pay for such a thing?*

Next, rewrite the following questions in more formal style, using simple or complex inversion as appropriate.

> **5** *Est-ce que vous avez eu de ses nouvelles?*
> *Have you heard from her/him?*
>
> **6** *Est-ce qu'elle vous a téléphoné?*
> *Has she phoned you?*
>
> **7** *Est-ce que le courrier est arrivé?*
> *Has the mail arrived?*

8 **Pourquoi est-ce que le livre n'est pas paru?**
Why hasn't the book been published?

9 **Qu'est ce que les étudiants en pensent?**
What do the students think about it?

10 **De quoi est-ce qu'il s'agit dans le film?**
What is the film about?

11 **Comment est-ce que le gouvernement va régler l'affaire?**
How is the government going to sort out the matter?

12 **Où est-ce que l'action se passe?**
Where does the action take place?

II   After direct speech

Verbs which follow a passage of direct speech and which are used to report the actual words which someone says are always inverted in written French (see Day 2, Section IV). Simple inversion is all that is required for this. For example:

> **«Je n'ai aucune idée», a-t-il dit.**
> ['I have no idea,' he said.]
> **«Vous en avez pour une demi-heure», précisa mon guide.**
> ['It will take you half an hour,' my guide added (added my guide).]

An optional inversion is sometimes used in English, but note that in French inversion is compulsory.

Rewrite the following sentences, putting the underlined words to the end of the sentence and making any other necessary changes.

13 **Le ministre demanda, «Où avez-vous trouvé ces documents?»**
'Where did you find these documents?' the minister asked.

14 **Elle cria: «Entrez».**
'Come in,' she shouted.

III   After *aussi, peut-être,* etc.

In careful, formal style, if you begin a sentence with one of the following adverbs, you should invert the verb and subject. Look at the examples:

à peine hardly	**Aussi les vacanciers sont-ils**
ainsi in that way	**partis.** So the holidaymakers left.
aussi so, therefore	**Peut-être pensaient-ils à autre**
du moins at least	**chose.** Perhaps they had
peut-être perhaps	something else in mind.
sans doute doubtless	**Toujours est-il que je ne peux**
toujours anyway, all the same	**pas vous aider.** The fact remains
	that I can't help you.

Three things to note:

- If there is a noun subject (see first example above), you must use complex inversion.
- In less formal French, an alternative to inversion after **peut-être** and **sans doute** is the insertion of **que**, followed by direct word order (subject, verb, complement). For example:

Peut-être qu'il a manqué son train.
[Maybe he has missed his train.]
Sans doute que vous avez raison.
[Doubtless you are right.]

- If **aussi** is placed at the beginning of a sentence, it does not mean 'also'!

Rewrite the following sentences, placing the adverb at the beginning and making any other necessary changes.

---

15 **Les écologistes ont sans doute raison.**
The ecologists are doubtless right.

16 **Elle est du moins restée dans les délais.**
At least she met the deadline.

17 **Il était à peine arrivé qu'il pensait déjà à repartir.**
No sooner had he arrived than he was thinking of leaving again.

18 **Ils manquent peut-être de personnel.**
Maybe they are short of staff.

IV   Optional uses of inversion for emphasis
The uses of inversion which you have studied so far are all more or less compulsory features of formal written style. In the remainder of today's study, you will focus on uses of inversion which are optional. In the following cases, it is simple inversion that is involved with both noun and pronoun subjects.

i) After adverbial expressions of time or place

If you wish to place particular emphasis on the subject rather than the verb, it is optional in formal style to use inversion after adverbial expressions of time or place. For example:

Ensuite arrivèrent les autres.
[Then the others arrived.]
De là résultent toutes nos difficultés.
[Hence all our difficulties.]

Rewrite the following sentences, placing the adverbs at the beginning of the sentence and using inversion of verb and subject.

---

19   *Tous vos problèmes découlent de là.*
       All your problems stem from here.

20   *L'automne, morne et pluvieux, arriva bientôt.*
       The autumn, rainy and dreary, soon arrived.

21   *Un nouvel obstacle survint ensuite.*
       A further obstacle then arose.

---

ii) Optional uses of inversion for reasons of balance

In formal written French, inversion frequently occurs in relative, comparative and concessive clauses, when the subject is longer than the verb. For example:

Ce que disent les hommes politiques est souvent hors de propos.
[What politicians say is often irrelevant.]
Il est plus intelligent que ne le pensent ses professeurs.
[He is more intelligent than his teachers think.]
Quelles que soient ses raisons, je ne peux pas l'excuser.
[Whatever her/his reasons may be, I cannot excuse her/him.]

This happens because there is a preference in French for putting short phrases before long ones, and for avoiding a monosyllabic verb at the end of a phrase or sentence. Try to observe this in your own writing; always read through what you have written to see whether you could improve the balance of your phrases/sentences by use of inversion.

Rewrite the following sentences, using verb–subject inversion in the subordinate clause.

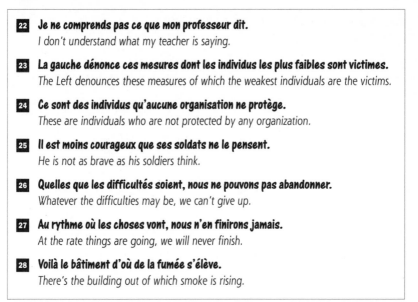

22 **Je ne comprends pas ce que mon professeur dit.**
I don't understand what my teacher is saying.

23 **La gauche dénonce ces mesures dont les individus les plus faibles sont victimes.**
The Left denounces these measures of which the weakest individuals are the victims.

24 **Ce sont des individus qu'aucune organisation ne protège.**
These are individuals who are not protected by any organization.

25 **Il est moins courageux que ses soldats ne le pensent.**
He is not as brave as his soldiers think.

26 **Quelles que les difficultés soient, nous ne pouvons pas abandonner.**
Whatever the difficulties may be, we can't give up.

27 **Au rythme où les choses vont, nous n'en finirons jamais.**
At the rate things are going, we will never finish.

28 **Voilà le bâtiment d'où de la fumée s'élève.**
There's the building out of which smoke is rising.

iii)   Inversion in other types of subordinate clause
You will also find inversion in other types of subordinate clauses. For example:

> **C'est aux pauvres que nuit cette mesure.**
> [It's the poor who are harmed by this measure.]
> **Je resterai tant que durera la grève.**
> [I'll stay for as long as the strike lasts.]

Again, this is something which you can try for yourself to improve the balance of your sentences.

Rewrite the following sentences, using verb–subject inversion in the subordinate clause.

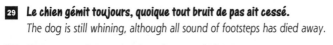

29 **Le chien gémit toujours, quoique tout bruit de pas ait cessé.**
The dog is still whining, although all sound of footsteps has died away.

30 **Tant que son époux vivait, elle était restée à Paris.**
For as long as her husband lived, she had stayed in Paris.

See for further information
Hawkins and Towell, 5.7.4, 14.3.5–14.3.7
Judge and Healey, Chapter 18, §3.1.2
Byrne and Churchill, §§583–4, 589–91, 596–601
Ferrar, §§63, 115, 133, 238

Key points:
Relative pronouns

DAY 20

Do you sometimes forget to use relative pronouns in French? That's because we often do omit them in English, e.g. 'the way he writes', 'the book she left on the train', 'the man I met yesterday'. But this is not possible in French, and it's one of the very basic things, along with adjective agreements and verb endings, for which you should always check your work methodically. The next thing is, which relative pronoun to choose!

I   Subject or object: *qui, que, qu'*

Do you sometimes hesitate between the relative pronouns **qui** and **que**, even though you know that **qui** refers to a noun/pronoun which is the subject of the verb in the relative clause and **que** refers to one which is the direct object? Often the problem is simply identifying which verb is relevant. It is the verb in the relative clause, not the verb in the main clause, which matters. In each of the example sentences below, the relative clause is italicized.

> **Est-ce que tu connais les gens *qui viennent d'entrer*?**
> [Do you know the people who have just come in?]

So, although **les gens** is the object of the verb **connais** in the main clause, it is the subject of the verb **viennent** in the relative clause, and the appropriate relative pronoun is therefore **qui**. Look at another example.

> **Elle prend le train *qui part à dix heures.***
> [She catches the train which leaves at ten o'clock.]

Here **le train** is the object of the verb **prend** in the main clause, but it is the subject of the verb **part** in the relative clause, so again the appropriate relative pronoun is **qui**.

Look now at an example where the relative pronoun **que** is required.

> **J'ai acheté le disque *que tu m'avais recommandé*.**
> [I have bought the record (which) you recommended to me.]

Here **le disque** happens to be the object of the verb **j'ai acheté** in the main clause, but this is irrelevant. What matters is that it is the direct object of the verb in the relative clause, **tu m'avais recommandé**. A second example makes clear how important it is to identify the right verb before deciding on **qui/que**.

La cathédrale *que nous avons visitée* **date du treizième siècle.**
[The cathedral (which) we visited dates from the thirteenth century.]

Here **la cathédrale** is the subject of the verb **date** in the main clause, but it is the object of the verb **nous avons visitée** in the relative clause, and so the appropriate relative pronoun is **que.** There is one very important difference between **qui** and **que** which you also need to remember. Before a vowel or inaspirate 'h', **qui never** elides to **qu'**, but **que** always does. For example:

Les gens qui habitent en face sont très sportifs.
[The people who live opposite are very keen on sports.]
La maison qu'ils ont achetée donne sur le parc.
[The house (which) they have bought looks over the park.]

Fill in the gaps with the appropriate relative pronoun: **qui, que,** or **qu'**.

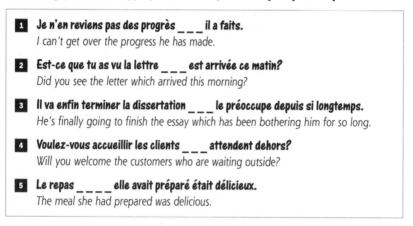

1 Je n'en reviens pas des progrès _ _ _ il a faits.
I can't get over the progress he has made.

2 Est-ce que tu as vu la lettre _ _ _ est arrivée ce matin?
Did you see the letter which arrived this morning?

3 Il va enfin terminer la dissertation _ _ _ le préoccupe depuis si longtemps.
He's finally going to finish the essay which has been bothering him for so long.

4 Voulez-vous accueillir les clients _ _ _ attendent dehors?
Will you welcome the customers who are waiting outside?

5 Le repas _ _ _ _ elle avait préparé était délicieux.
The meal she had prepared was delicious.

II *Dont*

Three reminders about **dont:**

* It can refer to people or to things. For example:

Voilà la femme dont je vous ai parlé
[There's the woman I spoke to you about. (of/about whom I spoke to you)]
Voici le livre dont je vous ai parlé.
[Here's the book which I spoke to you about. (of/about which I spoke to you)]

* Whenever the French construction involves **de**, the appropriate relative pronoun will be **dont**. So watch out for verbs which take **de**, especially when the English equivalent takes a direct object or a different preposition. For example:

le livre dont il a besoin/envie
[the book which he needs/wants] (**avoir envie/besoin de**)

le violon dont elle joue
[the violin which she plays] (**jouer** + **de** + musical instrument)
ses parents dont il dépend
[his parents on whom he depends] (**dépendre** + **de**)

Also watch out for prepositional phrases involving **de**. For example:

la façon/manière dont il parle
[the way (in which) he speaks] (**parler d'une telle façon**)

• If the verb in the relative clause has a direct object, it is not possible to place the object before the verb where it would be natural to do so in English, e.g. 'the secretary whose son I know'; 'an article, the title of which I have forgotten'. Before you translate into French, reword the relative clause in your mind, putting subject first, then verb, then the direct object. For example:

the secretary of whom I know the son
[la secrétaire dont je connais le fils]
an article of which I have forgotten the title
[un article dont j'ai oublié le titre]

Fill in the gaps in the following sentences with the appropriate relative pronouns. Notice how often the relative pronoun is omitted in the English translation. Remember that it can never be omitted in French.

> **6** *Je ne supporte pas la façon _ _ _ _ il parle.*
> *I can't stand the way he speaks.*
>
> **7** *J'ai oublié le dossier _ _ _ _ j'ai besoin.*
> *I've left the file I need behind.*
>
> **8** *C'est un film _ _ _ _ _ je me rappellerai toujours.*
> *C'est un film _ _ _ _ _ je me souviendrai toujours.*
> *That's a film I will always remember.*

Note the different verb constructions in sentence number 8:

On se rappelle quelque chose; On se souvient *de* quelque chose.

So, you will need a different relative pronoun with each verb.

Complete the following sentences. Be very careful about word order after the relative pronoun.

---

9   *C'est un ancien étudiant . . .*
He's a former student whose name I have forgotten.

10   *Voilà le spécialiste . . .*
That's the specialist whose address I gave you.

III   After prepositions

When prepositions other than **de** are involved, use preposition + **qui** for people. For example:

la femme à côté de qui j'étais assise
[the woman I was sitting next to]

In more formal English we would say 'the woman next to whom I was sitting'.

l'homme derrière qui il était assis
[the man he was sitting behind.]

The more formal version would be 'the man behind whom he was sitting'. This works for all prepositions except **entre** (between) and **parmi** (among). After these prepositions, you will need to use **lequel, lesquels, laquelle, lesquelles** to refer to people. For example:

les invités parmi lesquels il était assis
[the guests amongst whom he was sitting]

You will notice how often in informal English we omit the relative pronoun altogether and put the preposition at the end of the phrase. This is not an option in French. Before you translate into French, you need to rephrase the informal English into the more formal version.

When dealing with things rather than people, use preposition + **lequel,** but remember the following:

- It needs to agree as appropriate, **lequel**, **laquelle**, **lesquels**, **lesquelles**:

la porte devant laquelle il s'est arrêté
[the door outside which he stopped]

- In the masculine singular and in the masculine and feminine plurals, it combines with **à** to give **auquel, auxquels, auxquelles**. For example:

les adresses auxquelles il avait ecrit
[the addresses to which he had written]

- In the feminine singular it does not combine. For example:

l'université à laquelle elle s'est inscrite
[the university at which she registered]

Fill in the gaps with the appropriate relative pronoun.

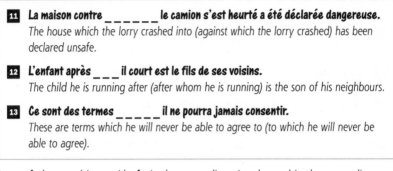

11 **La maison contre _ _ _ _ _ _ le camion s'est heurté a été déclarée dangereuse.**
The house which the lorry crashed into (against which the lorry crashed) has been declared unsafe.

12 **L'enfant après _ _ _ _ il court est le fils de ses voisins.**
The child he is running after (after whom he is running) is the son of his neighbours.

13 **Ce sont des termes _ _ _ _ _ il ne pourra jamais consentir.**
These are terms which he will never be able to agree to (to which he will never be able to agree).

Lequel also combines with **de** in the masculine singular and in the masculine and feminine plurals to give **duquel, desquels, desquelles**, but in the feminine singular, **de laquelle**, it does not combine. You will only ever need to use these forms instead of **dont** if there is another prepositional phrase present in addition to the one involving **de**. For example:

> **le pantalon dans la poche duquel j'ai oublié mes clefs**
> [the trousers in the pocket of which I have left my keys]

Fill in the gaps with the appropriate relative pronoun.

14 **Je ne pourrais pas supporter les odeurs de cuisine au milieu _ _ _ _ _ vous travaillez.**
I couldn't put up with the cooking smells which you work with (in the midst of which you work).

15 **Ce film passe au cinéma près _ _ _ _ _ il habite.**
This film is being shown at the cinema near to which he lives.

IV *Où* **as a relative**
Remember that a good and simple way to translate 'in/on which' is **où**. For example:

> **L'usine où il travaille est située de l'autre côté de la rivière.**
> [The factory in which/where he works is on the other side of the river.]

You may be less familiar with the use of **où** to refer to time. Avoid the common mistake of using **quand** or **lorsque** as a relative to translate such expressions as 'the day when'. You need to use **où** instead. For example:

> **Le jour où il est arrivé il pleuvait à verse.**
> [The day when he arrived it was pouring with rain.]
> **Au moment où il quittait le bureau, le téléphone a sonné.**
> [Just as he was leaving the office, the telephone rang.]

But if there is an indefinite article before **jour, moment,** etc., you need to use **que**. For example:

> **Un jour que je promenais le chien j'ai été témoin d'un accident.**
> [One day when I was walking the dog I witnessed an accident.]

Using **où** or **que** as appropriate, complete the following sentences.

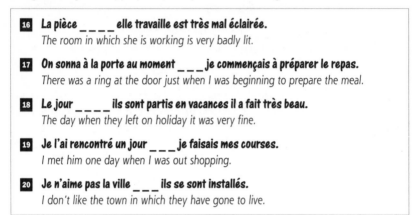

> **16** **La pièce _ _ _ _ elle travaille est très mal éclairée.**
> *The room in which she is working is very badly lit.*
>
> **17** **On sonna à la porte au moment _ _ _ je commençais à préparer le repas.**
> *There was a ring at the door just when I was beginning to prepare the meal.*
>
> **18** **Le jour _ _ _ _ ils sont partis en vacances il a fait très beau.**
> *The day when they left on holiday it was very fine.*
>
> **19** **Je l'ai rencontré un jour _ _ _ je faisais mes courses.**
> *I met him one day when I was out shopping.*
>
> **20** **Je n'aime pas la ville _ _ _ ils se sont installés.**
> *I don't like the town in which they have gone to live.*

V   *ce qui, ce que, ce dont*

Watch out for the three contexts in which you need to use **ce** before **qui**, **que**, **dont**:

- after the indefinite pronoun **tout**. For example:

  tout ce qui me plaît
  [everything I like (literally which pleases me)]
  tout ce qu'il aime
  [everything he likes]
  tout ce dont il a besoin
  [everything he needs]

  Be particularly careful with this, because in English we do not usually even use the relative pronoun 'which', let alone 'that which' – a literal translation of the French.

- To translate 'what', meaning 'the thing which'. For example:

  Ce que j'aime c'est la musique
  [What I like is music]

  You will practise this construction again on Day 26. It is used very frequently for highlighting/emphasizing a point.

- When you are referring back not to a single word, but to a whole idea or clause. For example:

Elle ne m'a jamais téléphoné, ce qui me surprend beaucoup.
[She has never rung me, which surprises me a lot.]

Fill in the gaps in the following sentences with the appropriate relative. In all cases but one, you will need a form beginning with **ce.** Can you spot the odd one out?

21 J'ai fait tout _ _ _ _ _ _ _je peux pour elle.
I have done all I can for her.

22 Elle m'a écrit une longue lettre, _ _ _ _ _ _ _ _ _m'a beaucoup surpris.
She wrote me a long letter, which greatly surprised me.

23 Elle lui a écrit une lettre _ _ _ _ _ _ l'a fait rire.
She wrote him a letter which made him laugh.

24 Est-ce que vous avez tout _ _ _ _ _ _ _ _ vous avez besoin?
Have you got everything you need?

25 _ _ _ _ _ _ _ _ _je voudrais vraiment faire ce soir, c'est aller au cinéma.
What I would really like to do this evening is to go to the cinema.

IV   General review

Test yourself on the whole of this unit by correcting the following sentences written by students. All the errors concern relative pronouns.

26 C'est une question auquelle les cinéphiles européens se préoccupent beaucoup.
It's an issue which European cinema buffs are greatly concerned about. (Note the construction: **se préoccuper** + **de** + noun)

27 Reste à savoir si les cinéastes réussiront à obtenir l'argent qu'ils en ont besoin.
It remains to be seen if film directors will get the money which they need.

28 Je vais expliquer les raisons pourquoi je ne suis pas partisan de cette affirmation préliminaire.
I will explain the reasons why I do not support this initial assertion. (Note: **On fait quelque chose pour des raisons particulières**)

29 Cette guerre des sexes remonte à l'époque lorsque les femmes ont soudain découvert leur liberté sexuelle.
This war of the sexes goes back to the time when women suddenly found their sexual freedom.

30 C'est qu'il y a de certain, c'est qu'il n'y arrivera jamais.
What is certain is that he will never manage it.

See for further information
Hawkins and Towell, Chapter 15
Jubb and Rouxeville, Chapter 11
Judge and Healey, Chapter 14
Byrne and Churchill, §§262–77
Ferrar, §§184–98

Key points: The infinitive and present participle

The infinitive has a wide range of uses in French and you will need to consult one of the reference grammars listed at the end of this unit if you want to review them all. You will be concentrating here on some of the most common problems which arise.

I   Use of the infinitive to translate an English present participle
Remember to use a French infinitive in the following cases where we would use a present participle (i.e. a verb form ending in '-ing') in English:

- After all prepositions, except **en**. For example:

  sans savoir
  [without knowing]
  avant de partir
  [before leaving]

  By contrast, note that the normal way of translating 'by + doing' is the preposition **en** which is followed by a present participle. For example:

  C'est en écrivant qu'on apprend à écrire.
  [It's by writing that you learn to write.]

  See Section III below for further practice with this.

  But note that after a verb of beginning/ending, you need to use the preposition **par** followed by an infinitive. For example:

  Il a commencé/terminé par dire . . .
  [He began/ended by saying . . .]

- As the complement to a noun, most commonly preceded by **de**. For example:

  façon de parler
  [way of speaking]
  manière de penser
  [way of thinking]
  défense de fumer
  [no smoking]

- After verbs of perception, such as **voir**, **entendre**, **(se) sentir**. For example:

Nous l'avons vu sortir de l'immeuble.
[We saw him leaving the building.]
Il l'a entendu rentrer après minuit.
[He heard him coming back in after midnight.]
Elle s'est sentie rougir.
[She felt herself blushing.]

- After **passer du temps (à)** and **rester (à)**. For example:

Ils ont passé toute la matinée à chercher ce dossier.
[They spent all morning looking for this file.]
Ils sont restés une heure à bavarder.
[They stayed for an hour chatting.]

Complete the following sentences.

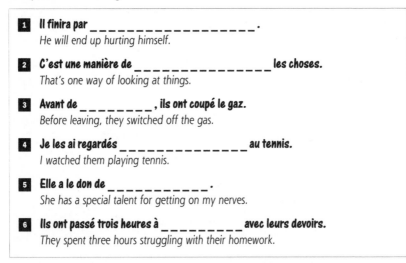

1 Il finira par _.
He will end up hurting himself.

2 C'est une manière de _ _ _ _ _ _ _ _ _ _ _ _ _ _ _ _ les choses.
That's one way of looking at things.

3 Avant de _ _ _ _ _ _ _ _ _, ils ont coupé le gaz.
Before leaving, they switched off the gas.

4 Je les ai regardés _ _ _ _ _ _ _ _ _ _ _ _ _ _ _ au tennis.
I watched them playing tennis.

5 Elle a le don de _ _ _ _ _ _ _ _ _ _ _ _.
She has a special talent for getting on my nerves.

6 Ils ont passé trois heures à _ _ _ _ _ _ _ _ _ avec leurs devoirs.
They spent three hours struggling with their homework.

Now correct the errors in the following sentences written by students, paying particular attention to the translation of the English verb which ends in -ing.

7 Est-il possible de contracter ce virus par manger du bœuf?
Is it possible to contract this virus by eating beef?

8 La famille passe la soirée en regardant la télévision.
The family spends the evening watching television.

II   Perfect infinitive after *après*

The preposition **après** is followed by a past infinitive, formed from the infinitive of the appropriate auxiliary, **avoir** or **être** (see Day 11) + past participle. For example:

> **Après s'être plaint au directeur, il est retourné à son travail.**
> [After complaining (After he had complained) to the manager, he went back to his work.]
> **Après avoir fait la sieste, il est sorti.**
> [After having a nap (After he had had a nap), he went out.]

Note that you can only use this construction if the subject in both halves of the sentence is the same. If it is not, you will have to use the conjunction **après que** (see Day 25, Section III). For example:

> **Après que je leur ai parlé, ils ont garé leur voiture ailleurs.**
> [After I spoke to them, they parked their car elsewhere.]

Complete the following sentences by using a perfect infinitive.

---

9 Après (lire) _ _ _ _ _ _ _ _ _ _ _ son rapport, je comprends mieux la situation.
After reading his report, I understand the situation better.

10 Après (terminer) _ _ _ _ _ _ _ _ _ mon travail, je suis allé me promener dans le parc.
After finishing my work, I went for a walk in the park.

11 Après (tomber) de cheval, elle a passé une semaine à l'hôpital.
After she fell off her horse, she spent a week in hospital.

III   The present participle and the gerund

Do you sometimes wonder whether or not you need to make the present participle agree? It only agrees if it is functioning as an adjective. For example:

> **une beauté rayonnante**
> [radiant beauty]
> **à une vitesse étourdissante**
> [at a dizzying speed]

If it is functioning as a verb, there is no agreement. For example:

> **La bouteille contenant la drogue est tombée à terre, éclatant en mille morceaux.**
> [The bottle containing the drug fell to the ground, shattering into a thousand pieces.]

In this example the noun object, **la drogue,** which follows the present participle **contenant** and the adverbial, **en mille morceaux**, which follows **éclatant** are sure signs that both these present participles are functioning as verbs and there is therefore no agreement in either case.

Make the present participles agree where necessary in the following sentences.

---

12 *C'est l'idéologie dominant.*
It is the dominant ideology.

13 *C'est une collection rassemblant des objets des quatre coins du monde.*
It's a collection bringing together objects from all corners of the world.

14 *Je ne trouve pas ses idées très convaincant.*
I don't find his ideas very convincing.

Apart from the agreement question, students' main problem with the present participle in French is usually deciding when to use it alone and when to use the gerund, i.e. the present participle preceded by **en**. Remember the following points:

• The present participle may function as the equivalent of a relative clause. For example:

On voit une file de voitures avançant (= qui avancent) très lentement.
[You can see a line of cars moving (which are moving) very slowly forward.]

• Alternatively, it may function as the equivalent of a causal clause. For example:

Etant infirmière (= comme elle est infirmière), elle sait faire le bouche à bouche.
[Being (because she is) a nurse, she knows how to do mouth to mouth resuscitation.]

• The gerund acts as an adverbial phrase of time or manner and often translates the English 'as', 'on', 'while' or 'by', 'in' + '-ing'. For example:

En faisant la vaisselle, elle pensait à la lettre qu'elle devait écrire plus tard.
[While doing the washing up, she was thinking about the letter which she had to write later.]
En disant cela, vous risquez de décourager les étudiants.
[By saying that, you are in danger of putting the students off.]

Fill in the blanks in the following sentences as appropriate with either the present participle or the gerund of the verb indicated.

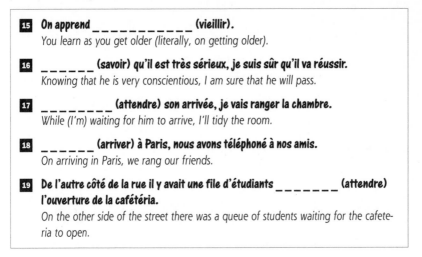

15 **On apprend _ _ _ _ _ _ _ _ _ _ (vieillir).**
You learn as you get older (literally, on getting older).

16 **_ _ _ _ _ _ (savoir) qu'il est très sérieux, je suis sûr qu'il va réussir.**
Knowing that he is very conscientious, I am sure that he will pass.

17 **_ _ _ _ _ _ _ _ (attendre) son arrivée, je vais ranger la chambre.**
While (I'm) waiting for him to arrive, I'll tidy the room.

18 **_ _ _ _ _ _ (arriver) à Paris, nous avons téléphoné à nos amis.**
On arriving in Paris, we rang our friends.

19 **De l'autre côté de la rue il y avait une file d'étudiants _ _ _ _ _ _ _ (attendre) l'ouverture de la cafétéria.**
On the other side of the street there was a queue of students waiting for the cafeteria to open.

Preceded by **tout**, the gerund may express the simultaneity of two actions. For example:

> **Tout en feuilletant le journal, elle écoutait les informations à la radio.**
> [While leafing through the newspaper, she was listening to the news on the radio.]

In a different context **tout** + gerund may have concessive force and be roughly equivalent to 'although'. For example:

> **Tout en voulant le croire, je trouve ses excuses peu convaincantes.**
> [While wanting to (Although I'd like to) believe him, I don't find his excuses very convincing.]

Complete the following sentences, using **tout** + gerund.

20 **_ _ _ _ _ _ _ _ _ _ _ _ _ _ _ _ _ _ _ assister au congrès, je ne peux vraiment pas me le permettre.**
Although I would like to attend the conference, I really can't afford it.

21 **_ _ _ _ _ _ _ _ _ _ _ _ _ _ , elle nous racontait des histoires.**
While she knitted, she told us stories.

IV   Translating English phrasal verbs with a gerund

Do you have problems translating English phrasal verbs of movement, e.g. 'He ran across the road'? Whereas we use a verb to express the manner of movement and a preposition to express the direction, in French you need a verb to express the direction of the movement and an adverbial to express the manner. For example:

Il traversa la rue en courant.
[He ran across the road.]

The gerund is often a very useful adverbial in such contexts.

Complete the following sentences. In each case, you will need to combine one of the verbs from list A (in the appropriate passé composé form) with a gerund from list B.

List A	List B
s'avancer, partir, monter	**en boitant, en rampant, en courant**

Note that the verb **monter** takes the auxiliary **avoir** when it is followed by a direct object. For example:

Il a monté la colline.
[He climbed the hill.]

---

22 **Dès qu'il a vu la police, il** _ _ _ _ _ _ _ _ _ _ _ _ _ _ _ _ _ _ **.**
As soon as he saw the police, he ran off.

23 _ **vers la porte.**
He limped forward towards the door.

24 **J'** _ _ _ _ _ _ _ _ _ _ _ _ _ _ **l'escalier** _ _ _ _ _ _ _ _ **.**
I crawled up the stairs.

V   The subjunctive to translate an English infinitive

Do you sometimes fall into the trap of translating an English infinitive in a sentence like 'He wants us to leave' with a French infinitive? Many students forget that when the subject of the two verbs is different, it is impossible to translate the second verb by an infinitive. Instead you need to use a subjunctive. For example:

Il veut que nous partions.
[He wants us to leave.]

Watch out particularly for this problem in the following cases:

• After verbs expressing desire/preference, such as **désirer**, **aimer** (**mieux**), **préférer**. For example:

Je préfère que vous restiez là.
[I prefer you to stay there.]

- After impersonal verbs expressing necessity, such as **il faut, il est nécessaire**. For example:

Faut-il que je lui écrive maintenant?
[Is it necessary for me to (Must I) write to him now?]

Complete the following sentences. Remember that if the subject of both verbs in the sentence is the same, you should use an infinitive for the second verb; if the verbs have different subjects, you will need to use a subjunctive.

---

25 **Je préfère** _ _ _ _ _ _ _ _ _ _ _ **seul.**
I prefer to work on my own.

26 **Je préfère** _ _ _ _ _ _ _ _ _ _ _ _ _ _ _ _ _ _ _ **seuls.**
I prefer them to work on their own.

27 **Elle veut** _ _ _ _ _ _ _ _ _ _ _ _ _ _ _ _ _ **les voir la semaine prochaine.**
She wants us to call to see them next week.

28 **Je voudrais** _ _ _ _ _ _ _ _ _ _ _ _ _ _ _ _ _ _ **les voir la semaine prochaine.**
I would like to call to see them next week.

29 **Est-il vraiment nécessaire** _ _ _ _ _ _ _ _ _ _ _ _ **à Londres?**
Is it really necessary for you to go to London?

30 **Il est essentiel de** _ _ _ _ _ _ _ _ _ _ _ **les épreuves avec beaucoup de soin.**
It is essential to check the proofs very carefully.

See for further information
Hawkins and Towell, 11.1.3, 11.1.5, Chapter 12, 17.6–17.9.4
Jubb and Rouxeville, Chapters 20, 24
Judge and Healey, Chapter 8, §§1, 3, 4
Byrne and Churchill, §§425–6, 482
Ferrar, §§25–37, 44–5

Upgrade your style: Logical connectors

DAY 22

It is important to be able to structure your ideas in French using appropriate signposts and connecting expressions.

I Signposting and sequencing

Whether you are giving an oral presentation or writing a report, it is essential to signal to your audience the stages in your argument. Try to include the following expressions in your active vocabulary.

Opening

d'abord firstly
tout d'abord first of all
en premier lieu in the first place
dans un premier temps first

Sequencing

ensuite next
deuxièmement secondly
en second lieu secondly
dans un deuxième temps subsequently

Ending

en dernier lieu lastly
dans un dernier temps finally
en conclusion in conclusion
pour conclure; pour terminer in conclusion
en fin de compte at the end of the day
tout compte fait when all is said and done
en définitive when all is said and done

Fill in the gaps in the following sentences, using appropriate expressions from the list above.

> **1** Je voudrais _ _ _ _ _ _ _ _ _ _ _ _ _ _ _ _ _ _ vous remercier de m'avoir invité à prendre la parole.
> *I would like first of all to thank you for having invited me to speak to you.*

> **2** Dans un premier _ _ _ _ _ _ _ _ nous allons examiner les arguments des pro-Européens.
> *First, we will consider the arguments of the pro-Europeans.*

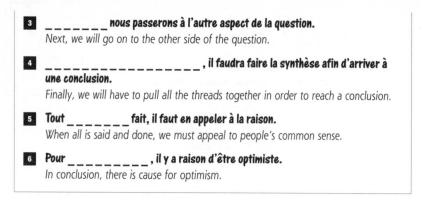

3 _ _ _ _ _ _ _ **nous passerons à l'autre aspect de la question.**
Next, we will go on to the other side of the question.

4 _ _ _ _ _ _ _ _ _ _ _ _ _ _ _ _ _ **, il faudra faire la synthèse afin d'arriver à une conclusion.**
Finally, we will have to pull all the threads together in order to reach a conclusion.

5 **Tout** _ _ _ _ _ _ _ **fait, il faut en appeler à la raison.**
When all is said and done, we must appeal to people's common sense.

6 **Pour** _ _ _ _ _ _ _ _ _ **, il y a raison d'être optimiste.**
In conclusion, there is cause for optimism.

II Linking ideas – alternatives to et

Used alone to link two ideas, **et** can be rather weak. There are various ways in which you can reinforce it. For example:

> **La vie urbaine est anonyme et stressante.**
> [Urban life is impersonal and stressful.]
> **La vie urbaine est anonyme et, qui plus est, stressante.**
> **La vie urbaine est anonyme et, plus important encore, stressante.**

Alternatively, you can use one of the following expressions.

à la fois ... et (see also Day 12, Section I), e.g. **pour des raisons à la fois culturelles et sociales**
[for cultural and social reasons]

aussi ... que, e.g. **Sa dissertation est aussi difficile à lire qu'à comprendre.**
[His essay is as hard to read as it is to understand.]

aussi bien que, e.g. **Cet article concerne les femmes aussi bien que les hommes.**
[This article concerns women as well as men.]

comme, e.g. **Ils sont paresseux, lui comme elle.**
[They're both as lazy as one another.]

non seulement mais aussi, e.g. **La vie urbaine est non seulement anonyme, mais aussi stressante.**
[City life is not just impersonal, but also stressful.]

Rewrite the following sentences, finding a suitable way either to reinforce or replace the conjunction **et**.

> **7** **Ce type d'argument est difficile à prouver et à réfuter.**
> *This type of argument is difficult to prove and to refute.*
>
> **8** **La piscine est ouverte en été et en hiver.**
> *The swimming pool is open in summer and in winter.*
>
> **9** **Les employés sont surmenés et sous-payés.**
> *The employees are overworked and underpaid.*
>
> **10** **Ce problème touche les jeunes et les vieux.**
> *This problem affects young and old.*
>
> **11** **C'est le symbole de la vie et de l'espoir.**
> *It is the symbol of life and hope.*
>
> **12** **Les hommes politiques, de droite et de gauche, ont donné des réponses évasives.**
> *Politicians, both right-wing and left-wing, have given evasive answers.*

III Logical sequence

There are a number of ways in which you can ring the changes on **donc** to express the idea 'so', 'therefore'.

ainsi thus, so then **aussi** + inversion of verb and subject 　(see Day 19, Section III) so, 　therefore	**c'est pourquoi** so (= that's why) **d'où** hence, from which **par conséquent** therefore, as a 　result

Complete the following sentences, using appropriate expressions from the list above.

> **13** **L'accusé n'a pas répondu, _ _ _ _ l'on peut tirer ses propres conclusions.**
> *The accused did not reply, from which we can draw our own conclusions.*
>
> **14** **Elle a beaucoup travaillé, _ _ _ _ _ a-t-elle réussi.**
> *She worked hard, so she succeeded.*
>
> **15** **Il paraît que vous n'avez pas reçu ma dissertation, _ _ _ _ _ _ _ _ _ _ je vous en envoie un double.**
> *Apparently you didn't receive my essay, so (= that's why) I'm sending you another copy of it.*
>
> **16** **_ _ _ _ _ _ _ _ , vous refusez de m'aider?**
> *So, you refuse to help me?*

Try also to ring the changes on **parce que** for 'because'. Consider the following possibilities.

attendu que given, considering that	**étant donné que** given that
dès lors que (formal French) since	**puisque** since
(Note that **dès lors que** also has	**vu que** in view of the fact that
a temporal meaning, 'as soon as')	

Complete the following sentences, using appropriate expressions from the list above.

17 **Réduire les allocations accordées aux mères-célibataires serait une mesure des plus réactionnaires, _ _ _ _ _ _ _ _ cela remettrait en question le droit des femmes à être indépendantes financièrement.**

Reducing the allowances given to single mothers would be a very reactionary step, since it would call into question the right of women to be financially independent.

18 **_ _ _ _ _ _ _ _ _ _ _ _ _ vous vous êtes excusé auprès du directeur, vous n'avez rien à craindre.**

Given that you have apologized to the manager, you have nothing to fear.

19 **_ _ _ _ _ _ _ _ _ _ il est déjà dix-huit heures, je propose que nous nous arrêtions là.**

In view of the fact that is it already six o'clock, I suggest that we call it a day.

20 **Dès _ _ _ _ _ _ que vous m'avez averti du problème, je m'en méfierai.**

Since you have forewarned me of the problem, I will be on my guard against it.

IV   Contrasting/Opposing

There are also a number of alternatives to **mais**. It may be possible to use a concessive. Look at these examples:

cependant however	word in a sentence, e.g. **C'était**
certes admittedly, e.g. **Certes, je**	**pourtant une bonne idée**. And
me suis trompé, mais.	yet it was a good idea; It was a
Admittedly, I made a mistake,	good idea, though.)
but . . .	**toutefois** however
Elle est intelligente, certes, mais	**bien que, quoique** (followed by the
paresseuse. She is intelligent,	subjunctive) – although, e.g. **Bien**
certainly, but she is lazy.	**que vous ayez raison, il**
et néanmoins but nevertheless	**vaudrait mieux vous taire**.
pourtant and yet, however, though.	Although you are right, it would be
(This often occurs as the second	better to keep quiet.

Rewrite the following sentences, replacing **mais** with a suitable expression from the list above, and making any other necessary changes.

> **21** **L'examen est difficile, mais pas impossible.**
> The examination is difficult, but not impossible.
>
> **22** **Il a été très gentil, mais j'ai un reproche à lui faire.**
> He has been very kind, but I have one criticism to make.
>
> **23** **Ce travail prend du temps, mais il n'est pas difficile.**
> This work takes time, but it isn't difficult.
>
> **24** **Il le sait, mais il ne veut pas l'admettre.**
> He knows, but he will not admit it.

Or, you could sometimes use one of the following expressions to contrast/oppose different ideas.

au contraire on the contrary	**par contre** on the other hand
contrairement à contrary to	**alors que** whereas
en revanche on the other hand	**tandis que** whereas

Rewrite the following sentences, replacing **mais** by a suitable expression from the list above, and making any other necessary changes.

> **25** **Il y en a qui sont favorables à une reconnaissance des spécificités insulaires, mais rares sont les élus qui ont prononcé ouvertement le mot autonomie.**
> There are those who are in favour of giving recognition to what is unique about the island, but there are few MPs who openly uttered the word autonomy.
>
> **26** **Le produit national brut du Japon augmente d'année en année, mais celui de la Grande-Bretagne est constamment en baisse.**
> The gross national product of Japan goes up year by year, but Great Britain's is continually going down.

V *Or*

Finally, a conjunction which is often overlooked by students. It is used in formal spoken and in written French. Try to use it in your own oral presentations and written work. Remember that it has three different functions:

- To indicate an opposition, roughly equivalent to 'and yet'. For example:

Elle m'a dit qu'elle serait dans son bureau, or elle n'y était pas.
[She told me she would be in her office, but (and yet) she wasn't there.]

- To introduce a new element, often translating English 'now', or 'as it happened'. For example:

La bibliothèque est fermée le lundi, or c'était justement un lundi que j'y suis allée.
[The library is closed on Mondays, and it just so happened that I went there on a Monday.]

It frequently introduces the next step in a logical argument, particularly when the argument moves from a general observation to a particular example. For example:

Tous les hommes sont mortels, or je suis un homme, donc je suis mortel.
[All men are mortal, (now) I am a man, therefore I am mortal.]

Note that in such a case, **or** is not usually translated into English at all.

- To conclude or recapitulate an argument, usually followed by **donc**. For example:

Or donc, il n'y avait pas d'autre solution.
[So then, there was no other answer.]

Translate the following sentences into English, and indicate in each case which of the three functions described above **or** is fulfilling.

---

27   Elle dit avoir passé la soirée à la bibliothèque, or personne ne l'y a vue.

28   Nous avons consulté tous les articles sans y trouver la référence requise. Or donc, il a fallu avouer notre échec.

29   On aurait dû vérifier les documents, or personne n'y a pensé.

30   J'avais déjà écrit une dissertation sur la politique étrangère de de Gaulle, or c'était le premier sujet de l'examen.

Key points: Modal verbs

DAY 23

*Do you have problems deciding how to translate English 'will', 'would', 'can', 'could', 'may', 'might', 'ought to', 'should', 'should have' and 'must' into French? Often it is a question of choosing the appropriate tense of a French modal verb, **vouloir, pouvoir, devoir**, but sometimes this won't do and you need to be aware of other possibilities.*

I ***Vouloir* and other possibilities for 'will' and 'would'**

i) *'Will'*

- Most commonly, of course, 'will' simply refers to future events and you translate it into French with a future tense of the appropriate verb or with **aller** + infinitive. For example:

 Nous partirons demain.
 [We will leave tomorrow.]
 Il va se faire mal s'il ne fait pas attention.
 [He will hurt himself if he isn't careful.]

- It is only appropriate to use a tense of **vouloir** to translate 'will' if an expression of wanting or wishing is involved. For example:

 Fais ce que tu veux.
 [Do as you will.]
 Est-ce que vous voulez une tasse de thé?
 [Will you have a cup of tea?]

ii) *'Would'*

- Most commonly, 'would' is a conditional form (see Day 9) and you need to use the conditional in French to translate it. For example:

 J'irais à Londres si j'avais le temps.
 [I would go to London if I had time.]

- Sometimes it is equivalent to 'used to', and refers to a habitual action in the past. In this case, you use the imperfect tense in French to translate it. For example:

Quand j'étais petite, je passais souvent l'après-midi chez ma grand'mère.
[When I was young, I would often spend the afternoon at my grandmother's.]

- It is only appropriate to use **vouloir** if 'would' expresses wanting or not wanting to do something. For example:

Voudriez-vous quelque chose à manger?
[Would you like something to eat?]
Il n'a pas voulu m'aider.
[He wouldn't (= was not willing/refused to) help me.]
Elle ne voulait rien entendre.
[She just wouldn't listen.]

Complete the following sentences, translating 'will' or 'would' as appropriate.

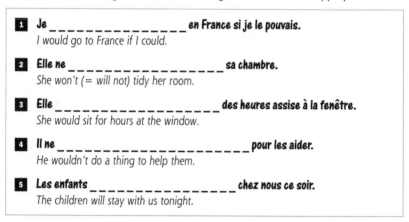

1 Je _ _ _ _ _ _ _ _ _ _ _ _ _ _ _ _ _ **en France si je le pouvais.**
I would go to France if I could.

2 Elle ne _ _ _ _ _ _ _ _ _ _ _ _ _ _ _ _ _ _ **sa chambre.**
She won't (= will not) tidy her room.

3 Elle _ _ _ _ _ _ _ _ _ _ _ _ _ _ _ _ _ _ _ **des heures assise à la fenêtre.**
She would sit for hours at the window.

4 Il ne _ **pour les aider.**
He wouldn't do a thing to help them.

5 Les enfants _ _ _ _ _ _ _ _ _ _ _ _ _ _ _ _ _ **chez nous ce soir.**
The children will stay with us tonight.

II   'should' and 'should have'

- If 'should' indicates a moral obligation, equivalent to 'ought to', then you use the conditional of **devoir** to translate it into French. For example:

Tu devrais faire attention.
[You should (ought to) be careful.]

- But beware of cases when 'should' is the equivalent of 'would'. You need to use the conditional of the relevant verb in such cases. For example:

Si j'avais plus d'argent, je m'achèterais un portable.
[If I had more money, I should (= would) treat myself to a laptop.]

- Occasionally English 'should' is the equivalent of a present tense, and is translated by a present-tense verb in French. For example:

Si vous le voyez, dites-lui bonjour de ma part.
[If you (should) see him, give him my best wishes.]

Complete the following sentences, translating 'should' as appropriate to the context.

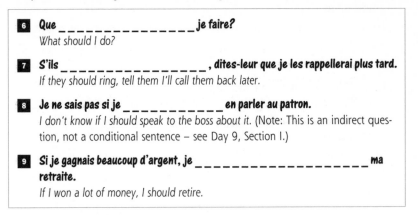

6 **Que _ _ _ _ _ _ _ _ _ _ _ _ _ _ _ _ je faire?**
What should I do?

7 **S'ils _ _ _ _ _ _ _ _ _ _ _ _ _ _ _ _ _ , dites-leur que je les rappellerai plus tard.**
If they should ring, tell them I'll call them back later.

8 **Je ne sais pas si je _ _ _ _ _ _ _ _ _ _ _ en parler au patron.**
I don't know if I should speak to the boss about it. (Note: This is an indirect question, not a conditional sentence – see Day 9, Section I.)

9 **Si je gagnais beaucoup d'argent, je _ _ _ _ _ _ _ _ _ _ _ _ _ _ _ _ _ _ _ ma retraite.**
If I won a lot of money, I should retire.

In the case of 'should have', if moral obligation, equivalent to 'ought to have', is expressed, you use the past conditional of **devoir**. For example:

Vous auriez dû le quitter.
[You should have left him.]

It is also possible to use the past conditional of the impersonal verb **falloir**. For example:

Il aurait fallu le quitter.
[You should have left him.]

What you should note in both cases is that you must use a past conditional followed by a present infinitive. Do not be tempted to use the present conditional followed by a past infinitive (***Vous devriez l'avoir quitté**). This is a common mistake, so be very careful!

Finally, 'should have' is sometimes simply the equivalent of 'would have' and is translated by a past conditional of the relevant verb in French. For example:

Si j'avais eu le temps, je serais allé au musée.
[If I had had time, I should (= would) have gone to the museum.]

Correct the errors in the following sentences.

10 **Je ne devrais pas avoir quitté la maison.**
I should never have left the house.

11 **Si j'étais rentré plus tôt, j'aurais dû préparer le repas.**
If I had got home earlier, I should (= would) have prepared the meal.

12 **Vous ne devriez pas être resté aussi longtemps.**
You should not have stayed so long.

III 'Could'

This causes frequent problems for English-speaking students.

- If 'could' expresses possibility, you will normally use the conditional of **pouvoir**. For example:

  Cela pourrait être une erreur.
  [That could be a mistake.]

- In a polite request, use the conditional of **pouvoir**. For example:

  Pourriez-vous me le faire savoir dès que possible?
  [Could you let me know as soon as possible?]

- Otherwise, the simplest solution is often to try a rephrasing exercise. If 'could' is the equivalent of 'was/were able to' then you need to use a past tense of **pouvoir** (imperfect or passé composé, depending on the context), but if it is the equivalent of 'would be able to', then you need the conditional of **pouvoir**. For example:

  Il ne pouvait pas/il n'a pas pu assister au congrès.
  [He couldn't (wasn't able to) attend the conference.]
  Il pourrait nous aider s'il le voulait.
  [He could (= would be able to) help us if he wanted to.]

  See also Day 9, Section II for this problem when it arises in conditional sentences.

Choose the appropriate tense of **pouvoir** to fill the gaps in the sentences below.

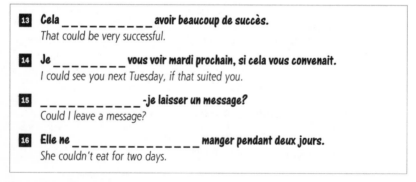

13 Cela _ _ _ _ _ _ _ _ _ _ avoir beaucoup de succès.
That could be very successful.

14 Je _ _ _ _ _ _ _ _ vous voir mardi prochain, si cela vous convenait.
I could see you next Tuesday, if that suited you.

15 _ _ _ _ _ _ _ _ _ _ _ -je laisser un message?
Could I leave a message?

16 Elle ne _ _ _ _ _ _ _ _ _ _ _ _ _ manger pendant deux jours.
She couldn't eat for two days.

IV 'may' and 'might'

If 'may' indicates permission or possibility, there is no problem about using the present tense of **pouvoir** to translate it. For example:

> **Tu peux sortir ce soir.**
> [You may (have permission to) go out this evening.]
> **Cela peut arriver.**
> [That may (possibly) happen.]

You should be on your guard for cases where you need a French subjunctive of the main verb instead of **pouvoir**. This often happens in a subordinate clause after an expression which triggers the subjunctive in French. Watch out particularly for the conjunctions **bien que, quoique** (although), universal expressions, such as **quoi que** (whatever) and verbs of fearing. For example:

> **Bien qu'il soit malade, il continue à travailler.**
> [Although he may be ill, he is still working.]
> **Quoi que tu en penses, j'y vais quand même.**
> [Whatever you may think of it, I'm going there all the same.]
> **J'ai peur qu'elle ne tombe.**
> [I'm afraid that she may fall.]

Complete the following with either the present tense of **pouvoir** + infinitive or the present subjunctive of the main verb as appropriate.

---

17 Bien qu'il en _ _ _ _ _ _ _ _ besoin, il ne pourra pas se le permettre.
Although he may need it, he won't be able to afford it.

18 Vous _ _ _ _ _ _ _ _ _ _ _ _ _ _ _ _ _ _ comme vous voulez.
You may do as you will.

19 Je t'appellerai quoi qu'il _ _ _ _ _ _ _ _ _ _ _ _.
I'll call you come what may (= whatever may happen).

20 Ce médicament _ _ _ _ _ _ _ _ _ _ _ _ _ _ _ _ _ _ des réactions de somnolence.
This medicine may cause drowsiness.

21 Je crains qu'il ne _ _ _ _ _ _ _ _ _ _ _ _ _ une bêtise.
I'm afraid he may do something silly.

Similar problems arise with the translation of 'might'.

- If 'might' indicates permission in indirect speech, you will translate it with the imperfect tense of **pouvoir**. For example:

  J'ai dit qu'ils pouvaient aller au cinéma ce soir.
  I said they might go to the cinema tonight.

- If it expresses possibility, use the conditional of pouvoir. For example:

  Cela **pourrait** arriver.
  [That might happen.]

- Otherwise, as with 'may', be on your guard for cases where you need a subjunctive of the main verb. For example:

  Elle avait peur qu'il ne lui arrive un accident.
  [She was afraid that he might have an accident.]

Complete the following with either an appropriate form of **pouvoir** or the present subjunctive of the main verb as appropriate.

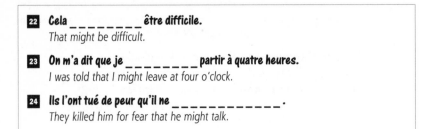

> **22** **Cela _ _ _ _ _ _ _ _ être difficile.**
> *That might be difficult.*
>
> **23** **On m'a dit que je _ _ _ _ _ _ _ _ partir à quatre heures.**
> *I was told that I might leave at four o'clock.*
>
> **24** **Ils l'ont tué de peur qu'il ne _ _ _ _ _ _ _ _ _ _ _ _ _ .**
> *They killed him for fear that he might talk.*

V **'must and 'must have'**
* When 'must' expresses moral obligation, use the present tense of **devoir** or **il faut**. For example:

Vous devez y aller.
[You must go there.]
Il faut lui écrire.
[You must write to him.]

* When 'must' or 'must have' indicates a supposition/logical possibility, use the present or the passé composé of **devoir**. For example:

Son train doit être en retard.
[His train must be late.]
Elle a dû oublier le rendez-vous.
[She must have forgotten the meeting.]

Complete the following sentences using the appropriate tense of **devoir**.

> **25** **Il _ _ _ _ _ _ déjà le savoir.**
> *He must already know.*
>
> **26** **Il _ _ _ _ _ _ _ _ _ partir hier.**
> *He must have left yesterday.*
>
> **27** **Nous _ _ _ _ _ _ _ _ _ rester à la maison ce soir.**
> *We must stay at home tonight.*
>
> **28** **Ils _ _ _ _ _ _ _ _ _ _ _ aller à l'hôpital.**
> *They must have gone to the hospital.*

VI Avoid using *pouvoir*

If you can avoid a potential problem with modal verbs, do so! After verbs of perception: seeing, hearing, smelling, tasting, when in English we would say 'I can see', 'she could hear', the simplest and best thing to do in French is to use the appropriate tense of the main verb and not worry about **pouvoir** at all. For example:

> **J'entends un bruit de pas.**
> [I can hear the sound of footsteps.]
> **Elle voyait la Tour Eiffel.**
> [She could see the Eiffel Tower.]

Complete the following sentences as appropriate:

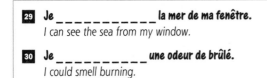

29 Je _ _ _ _ _ _ _ _ _ _ _ **la mer de ma fenêtre.**
I can see the sea from my window.

30 Je _ _ _ _ _ _ _ _ _ _ **une odeur de brûlé.**
I could smell burning.

See for further information

Hawkins and Towell, 11.2–11.3.7
Jubb and Rouxeville, Chapter 22
Judge and Healey, Chapter 4, §5.3.1, Chapter 6, §1.4, 1.5, 4.1–4.1.3
Byrne and Churchill, §§507–13, 529
Ferrar, §§64–9

Upgrade your style: Sentence openings

*One simple way to improve the style of your written French and give it a more authentic feel is to vary your sentence openings. You certainly don't have to start every sentence with the subject. If you pick up a piece of authentic written French and study two or three paragraphs, you may be surprised to find how many of the sentences start in other ways. You have already studied two of these: adverbials such as **peut-être, du moins** on Day 19, and logical connectors, such as **or** [and yet; now], **aussi** [so, therefore] on Day 22. Today you will be focusing on other possibilities which you may not always consider.*

I Expressions of time and place

You can give extra emphasis to expressions of time and place by placing them at the beginning of the sentence (see also Day 26 on highlighting and emphasis). For example:

> **Depuis son mariage, nous la voyons très peu.**
> [We haven't see much of her since she got married.]
> **A votre gauche vous verrez la cathédrale.**
> [You will see the cathedral on your left.]

Rewrite the following sentences, moving the expression of time or place to the beginning.

---

1 On trouve un petit marché sur la place.
There's a small market in the square.

2 Les Lyonnais ont illuminé leurs balcons de milliers de lampions ce jour-là.
The people of Lyons lit up their balconies with thousands of Chinese lanterns on that day.

3 On voit devant le restaurant un étalage alléchant de fruits de mer.
In front of the restaurant there is a mouthwatering display of seafood.

4 Le Premier Ministre a exposé son programme hier matin.
The Prime Minister outlined his programme yesterday morning.

> **5**   **Il y a des vendeurs de marrons chauds à chaque coin de rue.**
> *There are stallholders selling roast chestnuts on every street corner.*
>
> **6**   **Elle se laisse dépérir loin de sa famille.**
> *She is pining away from her family.*

II   Adjectives, adjectival phrases, past participles and nouns

You can start a sentence with an adjective, adjectival phrase, or a past participle used as an adjective. For example:

> **Fondée par l'évêque Elphinstone à la fin du quinzième siècle, l'université d'Aberdeen est l'un des plus anciens sièges du savoir de la Grande-Bretagne.**
> [Founded by Bishop Elphinstone at the end of the fifteenth century, the University of Aberdeen is one of the most ancient seats of learning in Britain.]

Note that even though it comes first, the adjective/participle still needs to agree with the subject (see Day 5). This construction is called an apposition, because the adjective/participle (qualified in this case by **'par l'évêque Elphinstone'**) is placed next to the subject. Such an apposition avoids the need to use a verb, and enables you to create a more compact and stylish sentence. If you had started with the subject, you would have had to use two clauses:

> **L'université d'Aberdeen qui a été fondée par l'évêque Elphinstone à la fin du quinzième siècle est l'un des plus anciens sièges du savoir de la Grande-Bretagne.**

Rewrite the following sentences using an adjective or past participle apposition to replace one of the clauses.

> **7**   **Elle s'arrêta parce qu'elle était fatiguée.**
> *She stopped becaue she was tired.*
>
> **8**   **Toulon a eté appelée durant la Révolution «Port La Montagne» et elle mérite bien cette dénomination.**
> *Toulon was called 'Mountain Port' during the Revolution and it well deserves this name.*
>
> **9**   **Elle est toute seule et elle sombre dans le désespoir.**
> *She is all on her own and sinking into despair.*
>
> **10**   **Ces îles sont isolées et sauvages et offrent un paysage magnifique.**
> *These islands are isolated and wild and present·some magnificent scenery.*

Try one more example, this time starting the sentence with an adjectival phrase in apposition.

---

11 **Le clocher est de style flamboyant et date du seizième siècle.**
The bell tower is late Gothic and dates from the sixteenth century.

It is also possible to start a sentence with a noun in apposition to the subject, once again gaining in concision. For example:

Siège du Conseil de l'Europe, Strasbourg est aussi capitale de l'Alsace.
[Headquarters of the Council of Europe, Strasbourg is also the capital of Alsace.]

Note that there is no definite or indefinite article with a noun in apposition.

Rewrite the following sentences using a noun apposition to replace one of the clauses.

12 **Montpellier est une ville accueillante et dynamique qui s'enorgueillit de nombreuses attractions touristiques.**
Montpellier is a welcoming and lively town which boasts many tourist attractions.

13 **La Sainte-Chapelle, qui est un chef-d'œuvre d'architecture gothique, est située dans l'enceinte du Palais de Justice.**
The Sainte-Chapelle which is a masterpiece of Gothic architecture, is situated within the compound of the Palais de Justice.

14 **Dijon est une ville historique qui nous a légué un certain nombre de jardins anciens.**
Dijon is a historic town which has left us a number of old gardens.

15 **Rouen est un grand centre industriel et c'est aussi un important centre commercial aux magasins fascinants.**
Rouen is a great industrial centre and it is also a major shopping centre with fascinating shops.

III Prepositional expressions
You can often start a sentence with a prepositional expression followed by a noun or pronoun. For example:

Face à cette situation, nous sommes partis plus tôt.
In view of this situation, we left earlier.

Rewrite the following sentences moving the prepositional expression to the beginning.

16   **J'ai écrit au rédacteur suite à l'article d'hier.**
I wrote to the editor following yesterday's article.

17   **Il ne peut rien faire sans elle.**
He can't do anything without her.

18   **Elle a démissionné en dépit de mes conseils.**
She resigned in spite of my advice.

19   **Ils ont réussi à force de patience.**
They succeeded through patience.

20   **Je suis parvenu à mon but grâce à elle.**
I achieved my goal thanks to her.

You can also begin a sentence with a preposition followed by an infinitive. For example:

> **Afin de finir à temps, il a dû raccourcir son discours.**
> [In order to finish on time, he had to cut short his speech.]

Rewrite the following sentences, moving the prepositional expression to the beginning.

21   **Il a baissé le volume afin de ne pas vous déranger.**
He turned down the volume so as not to disturb you.

22   **J'ai changé d'avis après l'avoir lu.**
I changed my mind after I had read it.

23   **Elle a relu la lettre avant de rédiger sa réponse.**
She re-read the letter before drafting her reply.

IV   Conjunctions

You can often begin a sentence with a conjunction, if you choose to start with the subordinate rather than with the main clause. For example:

> **Dès qu'il vous verra, il vous reconnaîtra.**
> [As soon as he sees you, he will recognize you.]

Rewrite, with the subordinate clause at the beginning:

24   **Il ne veut pas poursuivre ses études alors même qu'il le pourrait.**
He doesn't want to continue his studies even though he could.

25   **Elle s'amuse tandis que nous travaillons.**
She plays while we work.

26 **Elle ne travaille pas bien que les examens approchent.**
She is not working even though the exams are drawing near.

27 **Il a fermé le gaz de peur qu'il n'y ait une explosion.**
He switched off the gas for fear that there might be an explosion.

More ambitiously, it is also possible to begin a sentence with a conjunction such as **bien que** or **quoique** (although), followed by an apposition (see Section II above). For example:

> **Bien que chahutés à leur arrivée par les grévistes, les délégués ont exposé leur motion dans le calme.**
> [Although they were heckled by the strikers when they arrived, the delegates outlined their motion in peace and quiet.]

The apposition avoids the need for a subordinate clause, which in this case would have required a verb in the subjunctive.

Rewrite the following sentences, beginning with the conjunction **bien que**, followed by an apposition. Remember that it is possible to use an adjectival phrase, e.g. **de grande envergure** (far-reaching), in apposition (see sentence 11 above).

28 **La cathédrale Saint-Corentin est de faibles dimensions, comme toutes les cathédrales bretonnes, mais elle domine le paysage quimpérois.**
Saint Corentin's Cathedral is small in scale, like all Breton cathedrals, but it dominates the Quimper landscape.

29 **L'église est peu imposante, mais elle a une histoire mouvementée.**
The church is not very imposing, but it has an eventful history.

30 **Il est très jeune, mais il sait s'imposer.**
He is very young, but he knows how to assert himself.

See for further information
Jubb and Rouxeville, Chapter 28

*It is vital to be able to use conjunctions confidently, because otherwise you will not be able to build complex sentences, and your marks will reflect the limited range of your expression. You will be concentrating today on subordinating conjunctions. Co-ordinating conjunctions, such as **et** and **mais,** are more straightforward in that they are all followed by an indicative verb. In fact, the main problem with **et** and **mais** in particular is over-use, rather than under-use, as you saw on Day 22!*

I What is a conjunction?

English-speaking students sometimes have problems, because in English prepositions and conjunctions may have the same form, whereas in French they are different. For example:

> since (preposition) his arrival **depuis son arrivée**
> since (conjunction) he arrived **depuis qu'il est arrivé**

The key difference is that a conjunction is followed by a finite verb, i.e. a verb marked for tense and person. By contrast, a preposition is followed by a noun, pronoun, or non-finite verb (infinitive or participle). In French, the conjunction is often distinguished from the preposition by the addition of **que**. For example:

> **Il est parti avant la fin.**
> [He left before (preposition) the end.]
> **Parle-lui avant qu'il ne parte.**
> [Speak to him before (conjunction) he leaves.]

Read the following sentences and without translating them into French, note whether the underlined word is a preposition (P) or a conjunction (C).

> **1** He left <u>without</u> a word.
>
> **2** <u>After</u> she rang off, I remembered something I should have told her.
>
> **3** <u>Since</u> they arrived it has rained all the time.
>
> **4** He hasn't seen her <u>since</u> the accident.
>
> **5** <u>Before</u> he said anything, I could see he was not feeling well.
>
> **6** <u>Now</u> I know the parcel has arrived safely, I am happy.

II Conjunctions which are followed by the indicative

Many common conjunctions, including expressions of causality, such as **attendu que** [given that], **étant donné que** [given that], **parce que** [because], **puisque** [since], **vu que** [in view of the fact that], and the vast majority of conjunctions of time, such as **alors que** [when; whereas], **à mesure que** [as], **comme** [as], **aussitôt que**, [as soon as], **dès que** [as soon as], **lorsque**, **quand** [when], **maintenant que** [now that], **pendant que** [while], **une fois que** [once], are followed by a verb in the indicative. For example:

> **Maintenant que les billets sont arrivés nous pouvons partir.**
> [Now the tickets have arrived, we can set off.]

You need to be very careful, though, in your choice of tenses after conjunctions of time, because French usage does not always correspond to English usage.

• The future tense is used after conjunctions such as **aussitôt que, dès que, pendant que, tandis que** and after the even more common **quand** and **lorsque** when the verb in the main clause is in the future. For example:

Quand il arrivera, vous devrez lui expliquer ce qui s'est passé.
[When he arrives you will need to explain to him what has happened.]

Note that in English we would normally use the present tense in such circumstances.

• The future perfect is also used after the same conjunctions when the verb in the main clause is in the future. It translates an English perfect tense. For example:

Aussitôt qu'ils auront terminé, ils devront partir.
[As soon as they have finished, they will have to leave.]

Complete the following sentences with the verbs in the appropriate tense.

7 Quand je _ _ _ _ _ _ _ _ _ (finir) ma dissertation, je te donnerai un coup de fil.
When I've finished my essay, I'll give you a ring.

8 Le médecin vous verra dès que vous _ _ _ _ _ _ _ _ _ (arriver).
The doctor will see you as soon as you arrive.

9 Pendant que je _ _ _ _ _ _ _ _ _ (attendre), je rangerai quelques affaires.
While I'm waiting I'll tidy away a few things.

Similarly, the conditional is used after these same conjunctions when the verb in the main clause is in the conditional. In English we use the past tense in such cases. For example:

> **Il a dit qu'il nous ferait signe dès qu'il arriverait.**
> [He said he would let us know as soon as he arrived.]

Complete the following sentences with the verbs in the appropriate tense.

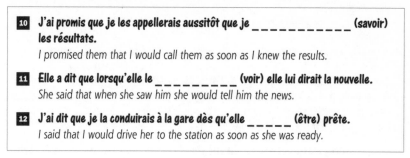

10 **J'ai promis que je les appellerais aussitôt que je _ _ _ _ _ _ _ _ _ _ (savoir)
les résultats.**
I promised them that I would call them as soon as I knew the results.

11 **Elle a dit que lorsqu'elle le _ _ _ _ _ _ _ _ _ (voir) elle lui dirait la nouvelle.**
She said that when she saw him she would tell him the news.

12 **J'ai dit que je la conduirais à la gare dès qu'elle _ _ _ _ _ (être) prête.**
I said that I would drive her to the station as soon as she was ready.

Finally, you should note that the rules for tense usage after the conjunction **depuis
que** (since) are the same as you learnt in Day 11, Section V with the preposition
depuis. In other words, if the action is ongoing at the time of reporting, French uses
a present tense where English uses a perfect, and an imperfect where English uses
a pluperfect. For example:

> **Depuis qu'elle étudie la médecine, elle a très peu de temps
> libre.**
> [Since she has been studying medicine, she has had very little free time.]
> **Depuis qu'elle étudiait la médecine, elle avait très peu de temps
> libre.**
> [Since she had been studying medicine, she had had very little free
> time.]

Complete the following sentences with the verbs in the appropriate tense.

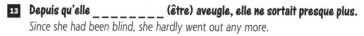

13 **Depuis qu'elle _ _ _ _ _ _ _ _ (être) aveugle, elle ne sortait presque plus.**
Since she had been blind, she hardly went out any more.

14 **Depuis qu'il _ _ _ _ _ _ _ _ _ _ _ (habiter) à Paris, je le vois très rarement.**
Since he has been living in Paris, I haven't seen much of him.

III   Conjunctions which are followed by the subjunctive
It is easier to remember which conjunctions are followed by the subjunctive if you
group them in your mind as follows:

- Three conjunctions of time: **avant que** [before]; **en attendant que** [until];
  jusqu'à ce que [until]. You will also increasingly find the subjunctive used after
  après que, though the grammar books will tell you that it should be followed
  by the indicative. For once you can't be wrong either way!
- Concessives: **bien que**, **quoique** [although], **malgré que** [despite the fact
  that].
- Expressions of purpose: **afin que**, **pour que** [in order that].

- Expressions of condition: **à condition que** [on condition that], **pourvu que** [provided that].
- Restriction, denial: **à moins que** [unless], **non que** [not that], **sans que** [without].
- Expressions of fear: **de crainte que**, **de peur que** [for fear that, lest].

Finally, there are three conjunctions, **de façon que**, **de manière que**, **de sorte que** [so that, in such a way that], which take either the indicative or the subjunctive, depending on whether they express an accidental result (indicative) or a deliberate purpose (subjunctive). For example:

> **Mon train est arrivé en retard de sorte que j'ai manqué le début de la conférence.**
> [My train arrived late so that (with the accidental result that) I missed the beginning of the lecture.]
> **J'ai pris le train de 7 heures de sorte que j'aie le temps de vous voir.**
> [I caught the 7 o'clock train so that (with the purpose that) I should have time to see you.]

Complete the sentences below with the verbs in the appropriate mood (indicative or subjunctive) and tense. You may need to check back to Section II above about use of tenses after conjunctions of time.

15   **Ils sont partis sans que je les _ _ _ _ _ _ (voir).**
They left without my seeing them.

16   **Avant que je ne leur _ _ _ _ _ _ _ (écrire), dites-moi ce que vous pensez de l'idée.**
Before I write to them, tell me what you think of the idea.

17   **Dès qu'il _ _ _ _ _ _ _ _ _ (rentrer), il voudra se reposer.**
As soon as he gets home, he will want to rest.

18   **Bien que je le _ _ _ _ _ _ _ _ _ (connaître) depuis longtemps, nous nous vouvoyons.**
Although I've known him for a long time, we call one another 'vous'.

19   **Ne lui en dis rien à moins que tu ne _ _ _ _ _ _ _ _ (vouloir) l'agacer.**
Don't tell him anything about it unless you want to annoy him.

20   **A mesure qu'elle _ _ _ _ _ _ _ (grandir), elle devenait plus sérieuse.**
As she grew up, she grew more serious.

21   **A condition que tu _ _ _ _ _ _ _ (faire) la vaisselle, je ferai la cuisine.**
On condition that you do the washing-up, I'll do the cooking.

22 Je lui téléphone régulièrement pour qu'elle _ _ _ _ _ _ (savoir) que je pense à elle.

I phone her regularly so that she knows I'm thinking about her.

23 On n'a pas rendu le livre à la bibliothèque de sorte que je ne _ _ _ _ _ _ (pouvoir) pas écrire ma dissertation.

The book hasn't been returned to the library so that I can't write my essay.

24 Une fois qu'ils _ _ _ _ _ _ _ _ _ _ _ _ _ (s'expliquer), il n'y avait plus de problème.

Once they explained themselves, there wasn't a problem any more.

25 Je ne veux pas la déranger de peur qu'elle ne _ _ _ _ _ _ _ _ (être) prise de panique.

I don't want to to disturb her lest she get into a panic.

IV With infinitives

Instead of using a conjunction followed by the subjunctive, it is often simpler and more natural in French to use a preposition followed by an infinitive if the subject of the subordinate clause is the same as the subject of the main clause. For example:

Avant de rentrer, je suis allé au supermarché.
[Before I went home, I went to the supermarket.]

Note that **avant** takes **de** before an infinitive. The following expressions: **afin de**, **à condition de**, **à moins de**, **de crainte de**, **de peur de** behave likewise. Other expressions: **jusqu'à**, **de manière à**, **de façon à**, **de sorte à** take **à** before an infinitive. That leaves **pour** and **sans** which can be used on their own before an infinitive. Finally, remember, as you saw in Day 21, Section II, that **après** is also followed directly by an infinitive, but it must be a perfect infinitive. For example:

Après avoir écouté les informations, je suis allé me coucher.
[After I had listened to the news, I went to bed.]

First correct the error in the following sentence written by a student.

26 Une femme peut retourner à son travail après elle a eu un enfant.

Then choose the most appropriate expression from the following list to fill in the blanks in the sentences below and note the use of the infinitive in each case rather than a conjunction followed by a verb in the subjunctive.

afin de, avant de, à condition de, à moins de

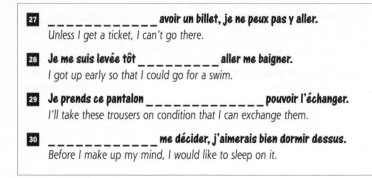

27 _ _ _ _ _ _ _ _ _ _ _ _ avoir un billet, je ne peux pas y aller.

Unless I get a ticket, I can't go there.

28 Je me suis levée tôt _ _ _ _ _ _ _ _ _ aller me baigner.

I got up early so that I could go for a swim.

29 Je prends ce pantalon _ _ _ _ _ _ _ _ _ _ _ _ _ pouvoir l'échanger.

I'll take these trousers on condition that I can exchange them.

30 _ _ _ _ _ _ _ _ _ _ _ _ me décider, j'aimerais bien dormir dessus.

Before I make up my mind, I would like to sleep on it.

See for further information
Hawkins and Towell, Chapters 13, 17
Jubb and Rouxeville, Chapters 26, 27
Judge and Healey, Chapter 5, §3.5, Part IV Link Words, Chapter 15
Byrne and Churchill, §§644–704
Ferrar, §§237–41, Appendix B

This is an important area of difference between French and English. In spoken English we can highlight a particular word simply by tone of voice, and/or by putting extra stress on it. In French, in both speech and writing, you need to make various changes to the 'normal' word order of subject + verb + object/complement.

I   Initial position

You have already seen on Day 24 that you can give extra emphasis to an adverbial expression or to an adjective, participle or adjectival phrase by placing it at the beginning of the sentence. It is also possible to highlight the direct object of a sentence by placing it at the beginning, but if you do this you will need to repeat the noun object in the form of a direct object pronoun later in the sentence. For example:

> **Ses petites manies, nous les connaissons très bien**.
> [We're very familiar with her little quirks.]

This repetition is sometimes called a *reprise* construction, and is particularly common in the spoken language.

Rewrite the following sentences, highlighting the underlined words by placing them at the beginning of the sentence and restructuring the rest of the sentence as necessary.

---

1 J'admire <u>mon amie</u> parce qu'elle est pleine d'entrain.
I admire my friend, because she is full of life.

2 Nous avons loué <u>notre appartement</u> à un collègue.
We have let our flat to a colleague.

3 Je vais corriger <u>ces copies</u> ce soir.
I'm going to mark these papers this evening.

Similarly, it is possible to place an infinitive complement at the beginning of the sentence, provided that you use an appropriate *reprise* construction later on. For example:

> **Travailler à l'étranger, elle y tient beaucoup**.
> [She's very keen on working abroad.]

Habiter en France, elle en rêve souvent.
[She often dreams of living in France.]

Take care with pronouns. Study the examples above and note the use of **y** for **à** + infinitive and **en** for **de** + infinitive (**tenir** + **à**; **rêver** + **de**).

Rewrite the following sentences, highlighting the underlined words by placing them at the beginning of the sentence and restructuring the rest of the sentence as necessary.

4 **Je n'ai pas le temps d'aller au théâtre.**
  I haven't time to go to the theatre.

5 **Elle tient beaucoup à apprendre le russe.**
  She's very keen to learn Russian.

6 **Ils ont vraiment envie de retourner en Amérique.**
  They really want to go back to America.

II Final position

The final position in the sentence may also be used for emphasis. Note the use of an appropriate pronoun to anticipate reference to the delayed noun. For example:

Il est trop cuit, ce gigot.
[This leg of lamb is overdone.]
Je l'ai fini, mon article.
[I have finished my article.]
Il y en a, des enfants.
[There are lots of children.]

Rewrite the following sentences, highlighting the underlined words by moving them to the end of the sentence, and restructuring the rest of the sentence as necessary.

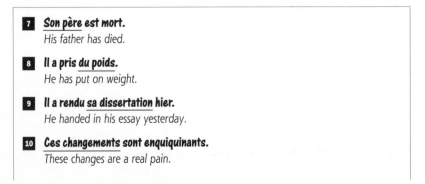

7 **Son père est mort.**
  His father has died.

8 **Il a pris du poids.**
  He has put on weight.

9 **Il a rendu sa dissertation hier.**
  He handed in his essay yesterday.

10 **Ces changements sont enquiquinants.**
  These changes are a real pain.

11 **Vous avez des problèmes.**
You have some problems. (Note: add emphasis without moving **problèmes**.)

12 **Cette femme se fait respecter.**
This woman commands respect.

III   Stressed pronoun

A stressed pronoun (**moi**, **toi**, **lui**, **elle**, **nous**, **vous**, **eux**, **elles**) may be added to emphasize a noun subject. It is usually placed immediately after the noun. For example:

Sa mère, elle, n'y consentira jamais.
[His/her mother will never agree to it.]

A stressed pronoun may also be used to highlight a pronoun subject. It may be placed in one of three positions in the sentence:

• at the very beginning, before the subject pronoun. For example:

Moi, je n'ai aucune idée.
[I have no idea.]

• immediately after the verb. For example:

Ils ne travaillent pas, eux, le dimanche.
[They don't work on Sundays.]

• at the end of the sentence,

Il n'a fait aucun effort, lui.
[He has made no effort.]

Make sure you remember the form of the masculine third-person plural stressed pronoun, **eux**. It is the one which students most frequently forget.

Rewrite the following sentences, adding a stressed pronoun to highlight the underlined words. Note that in some cases you will have a choice of position for the stressed pronoun.

13 **Ils ne travaillent pas assez.**
They don't work hard enough.

14 **Mon amie ne veut pas sortir ce soir.**
My friend doesn't want to go out this evening.

15 **Je ne comprends pas cet article.**
I can't understand this article.

16 **Vous prenez tout de travers.**
You take everything the wrong way.

17 **Nos voisins ne supportent pas le bruit.**
Our neighbours can't stand the noise.

18 **Il adore le sport.**
He loves sport.

IV   C'est qui/que

The framing device, **c'est . . . qui/que** is used very frequently to highlight a partic-ular element. This may be the subject. For example:

> **C'est le patron qui en décidera.**
> [It's the boss who will decide.]

It may be the object, direct or indirect. For example:

> **C'est son frère que nous avons vu.**
> [It was his/her brother that we saw.]
> **C'est à lui que j'ai donné l'argent.**
> [I gave the money to him.]

An adverbial phrase may also be highlighted in the same way. For example:

> **C'est à Madrid que j'ai acheté ce livre.**
> [I bought this book in Madrid.]

There are two further things to note about this construction.

• In careful French, you are advised to use **ce sont** with a plural noun. For exam-ple:

Ce sont nos voisins qui se sont plaints du bruit.
[It was our neighbours who complained about the noise.]

• The highlighting device may be used in the negative where appropriate. For example:

Ce n'est pas la seule chose qui compte.
[That's not the only thing which counts.]

Rewrite the following sentences, emphasizing the underlined words by using **c'est/ce sont ... qui/que** or the negative **ce n'est pas ... qui/que** as appropriate.

19 **Ils ont tenu parole.**
They have kept their word.

20 **Les étudiants ont tout organisé.**
The students have organized everything.

21 **On a offert le poste à Marie-Hélène.**
They have offered the job to Marie-Hélène.

22 **Je ne dois pas passer mon examen demain.**
I don't have to sit my exam tomorrow.

23 **Il fera du soleil à l'ouest.**
It will be sunny in the west.

24 **Je les ai vus hier.**
I saw them yesterday.

V   Ce qui, ce que, ce dont ... c'est/c'était

The relative pronouns **ce qui**, **ce que**, **ce dont**, followed by **c'est/c'était**, are frequently used to introduce the element of the sentence which you wish to highlight. For example:

> **Ce qui l'embêtait, c'était son impatience.**
> [What annoyed her was his impatience.]
> **Ce que je déteste, c'est remplir des tas de formulaires.**
> [What I hate is filling in piles of forms.]
> **Ce dont j'ai besoin, c'est d'un portable.**
> [What I need is a laptop.]

See Day 20, Section V if you need to revise the use of **ce qui**, **ce que**, **ce dont**.

Rewrite the following sentences, emphasizing the underlined words by using **ce qui/ce que/ce dont ... c'est/c'était**.

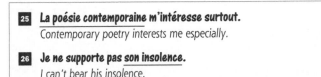

25 **La poésie contemporaine m'intéresse surtout.**
Contemporary poetry interests me especially.

26 **Je ne supporte pas son insolence.**
I can't bear his insolence.

27 **Faire la navette entre Paris et Lyon le fatiguait de plus en plus.**
Commuting between Paris and Lyons was increasingly tiring him.

28 **Elle aimait surtout <u>flâner dans le quartier latin</u>.**
She especially liked strolling in the Latin quarter.

29 **Vous aurez besoin d'<u>un parapluie</u>.**
You will need an umbrella.

30 **Elle déteste <u>faire la cuisine</u>.**
She hates cooking.

See for further information
Hawkins and Towell, 3.3, 5.7–5.7.4
Jubb and Rouxeville, Chapter 28
Judge and Healey, Chapter 12, §§5.2.2–5.3.2, 8.3–8.4
Byrne and Churchill, §§216, 255–6, 274, 633
Ferrar, §§115, 175

*If in doubt, you should always check in a dictionary or reference grammar to find out whether a French verb takes a straightforward direct object, takes an object introduced by **à** or **de**, or cannot take an object at all.*

I Transitive/intransitive verbs

A transitive verb is one which can take a direct object; an intransitive verb is one which cannot. You have already seen in Day 14, Section III, that the pronominal form of a French verb is often intransitive, while the non-pronominal form is transitive. For example:

Il s'est arrêté au carrefour.
[He stopped (intransitive) at the crossroads.]
Il a arrêté le véhicule.
[He stopped (transitive) the vehicle.]

In other cases, different verbs are used. The translation of the English 'to leave' is a case in point. Study the following examples.

Ils sont déjà partis.
[They have already left. (intransitive)]
Nous partons de la gare Saint-Lazare.
[We're leaving (intransitive) from the Gare Saint-Lazare.]
Il a quitté la France.
[He has left France. (transitive)]
Elle a quitté son mari.
[She has left her husband. (transitive)]
J'ai laissé un mot pour elle.
[I have left a message for her. (transitive)]
J'ai oublié mes clefs dans le train.
[I have left my keys on the train. (transitive)]

Complete the following sentences, choosing an appropriate verb.

---

1 Ils _ _ _ _ _ _ _ _ _ _ **pour Paris demain.**
They are leaving for Paris tomorrow.

2 Il a dû _ _ _ _ _ _ _ _ _ _ _ _ **quelque part pour déjeuner.**
He must have stopped somewhere for lunch.

3   **Les locataires ont _ _ _ _ _ _ _ _ _ l'appartement dans un état épouvantable.**
The tenants have left the flat in a dreadful state.

4   **Nous _ _ _ _ _ _ _ _ de chez nous à 19 heures.**
We're leaving home at 7 p.m.

5   **Ils vont _ _ _ _ _ _ _ _ _ _ l'école au mois de juin.**
They are going to leave school in June.

II   Verbs which take a direct object in French

You should always beware of thinking in English, and supposing that because an English verb needs a preposition before a noun, that the French translation equivalent will necessarily behave in the same way. For example, we look *at* something in English, but the French verb **regarder** takes a direct object. For example:

> **Elle regarde les photos de mariage de sa cousine.**
> [She is looking at her cousin's wedding photos.]

Watch out for other verbs like this.

approuver une décision to approve *of* a decision
attendre le bus to wait *for* the bus
chercher un dossier to look *for* a file
demander quelque chose to ask *for* something
écouter les informations to listen *to* the news
espérer une augmentation de salaire to hope *for* a pay rise
payer quelque chose to pay *for* something
regarder quelqu'un to look *at* someone
viser un marché particulier to aim *at* a particular market

Since all these verbs take a direct object in French, you will need to use direct object pronouns with them. For example:

> **Est-ce que vous avez écouté les informations. Oui, je *les* ai écoutées.**
> [Have you listened to the news? Yes, I have listened to it.]

Correct the errors in the following sentences.

6   **Il a payé cher pour sa réussite.**
He paid dearly for his success.

7   **Je lui ai regardé fixement.**
I stared at him.

> **8** **Il n'a pas rendu mon livre. Je vais lui en demander.**
> He hasn't returned my book. I'm going to ask him for it.
>
> **9** **Nous attendons pour le bus depuis une heure.**
> We're been waiting an hour for the bus.
>
> **10** **Ce project de loi vise aux chômeurs.**
> This bill is aimed at the unemployed.

III Verbs which take à + noun in French

The reverse also occurs. Some verbs take a direct object in English, whereas their translation equivalent in French takes **à** + noun.

aller à to suit	**plaire à /déplaire à** to
assister à un événement to attend	please/displease
(= be present at) an event	**renoncer à** to give up
convenir à to suit	**répondre à** to answer
nuire à to harm	**résister à** to resist
obéir à/désobéir à to obey/disobey	**ressembler à** to resemble, look like
penser à; songer à to consider	**survivre à** to survive
(= think about)	**téléphoner à** to phone

Remember to use indirect, rather than direct object pronouns with these verbs. For example:

> **Ce pantalon lui va très bien.**
> [Those trousers suit her very well.]
> **Elle lui ressemble beaucoup.**
> [She looks very like him.]
> **Il y a renoncé.**
> [He has given it up.]
> (See Day 17, Section V for use of the pronoun **y**.)

Correct the errors in the following sentences.

> **11** **Je vais le téléphoner ce soir.**
> I'm going to phone him this evening.
>
> **12** **Ce film les a beaucoup plu.**
> They like this film very much. (This film pleased them very much.)
>
> **13** **Cette crème résiste l'eau.**
> This cream is waterproof.

14 **Je n'en avais pas pensé.**
I hadn't considered (thought about) that.

15 **Il n'obéit pas les règles.**
He doesn't obey the rules.

IV   Verbs which take *de* + noun in French

Some other verbs which take a direct object in English are translated into French by a verb which takes **de** + noun.

s'apercevoir de to notice
s'approcher de to approach, get close to
avoir besoin de to need
avoir envie de to want
changer de to change (one thing for another of the same kind), e.g. **changer de pantalon** to change one's trousers
douter de to doubt
hériter de to inherit
jouir de to enjoy
manquer de to lack
se méfier de to distrust
se servir de to use
se souvenir de to remember
Remember to make appropriate use of pronouns, e.g. **J'en doute**. I doubt it.
    (See Day 17, Section IV for use of the pronoun **en**.)
Je me méfie d'eux. I don't trust them.
Les avantages dont il jouit sont considérables.
The advantages (which) he enjoys are considerable.

Rewrite the following sentences, replacing the underlined words with an appropriate pronoun.

16 **Est-ce que vous avez besoin de ce livre?**
Do you need this book?

17 **Je me souviens très bien de ces étudiants.**
I remember those students very well.

18 **Il doute de l'authenticité des documents.**
He doubts the authenticity of the documents.

Correct the errors in the following:

 La maison qu'elle a héritée est un véritable palais.
The house which she inherited is a real palace.

20 **Nous avons changé notre adresse.**
We have changed address. (We have moved to a new address.)

There are a number of other French verbs which take **de** + noun. Their English translation equivalents take a variety of different prepositions, such as 'on', 'for' and 'at'.

dépendre de to depend on   **rire de** to laugh at
remercier de to thank for   **vivre de** to live on

Correct the errors in the following sentences.

21 **Je te remercie pour cela.**
Thank you for that.

22 **Sur quoi vit-elle?**
What does she live on?

V   Verbs with two different usages
Distinguish carefully between the following.

jouer + **à** + sport, game, e.g. **jouer au football** to play football
jouer + **de** + musical instrument, e.g. **jouer du piano** to play the piano
penser + **à** to think about, of (= let one's thoughts dwell upon),
e.g. **Je pense à mes vacances.** I'm thinking about/of my holidays.
penser + **de** to have an opinion about,
e.g. **Que pensez-vous de son nouvel appartement?** What do you think of his new flat?
Be very careful, because in English we can use 'think of' in both senses.

Complete the following sentences with the appropriate preposition (**à/de**) or pronoun (**y/en**).

23 **Il joue très bien _ _ _ _ la flûte.**
He plays the flute very well.

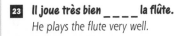

24 **Qu'est-ce que tu _ _ _ _ penses?**
What do you think of this?

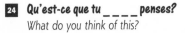

25 Maintenant que je_ _ _ _ pense, je suis sûr qu'il n'a pas parlé d'elle.
Now I come to think of it, I'm sure he didn't mention her.

26 Il faut penser _ _ _ _ votre carrière!
You must think of your career!

27 Ils jouent _ _ _ échecs.
They are playing chess.

VI   Verbs which take other prepositions
Note the following.

entrer dans to enter (+ direct object in English)	**se fâcher contre quelqu'un** to get angry with someone
consister en to consist of	

Correct the errors in the following sentences:

28 L'examen consiste de deux épreuves.
The exam consists of two papers.

29 Elle s'est fâchée avec lui pour un rien.
She got angry with him over nothing.

30 Nous l'avons vu entrer la maison par la fenêtre.
We saw him enter the house through the window.

See for further information
Hawkins and Towell, 8.1–8.5
Byrne and Churchill, §§ 519–26
Ferrar, §§50, 51, 56, 57

Accents, elision and capitalization

The points which you will be practising today are all relatively minor details, but if you get them right consistently, your French will make a much better impression.

I Use of accents
The aim here is to focus on some common problems. For a more systematic treatment, you will need to consult a reference grammar.

i) Acute and grave accents

- Don't use an **é** before '**s**' + another consonant, e.g. **esprit**, or before '**x**', e.g. **expédier**.
- There is no grave accent on the '**a**' in **ça/cela** (that). Don't confuse these with the expression **çà et là** (here and there).
- Remember to use a grave accent to distinguish the preposition **à** from the verb form **a,** and **où** (where) from **ou** (or).

Correct the errors in the following sentences, focusing on the use of accents. You should find one error in each sentence. If you find more, or can't find any at all, re-read the notes above and try again.

1. **Cela va au-delà de toutes mes ésperances.**
That's beyond my wildest dreams.

2. **Ou avez-vous trouvé une telle explication?**
Where did you find such an explanation?

3. **J'hésite a vous déranger.**
I hesitate to disturb you.

4. **Çà y est, ça recommence!**
Here we go again!

ii) The circumflex accent

- Remember to use a circumflex accent to distinguish **dû** (past participle of **devoir**) from **du** (= **de** + **le**).

- Be careful with verbs ending in -**aître**, e.g. **connaître, paraître**. You only need a circumflex on the '**i**' when it is followed immediately by a '**t**'. This happens in the third-person singular of the present tense, e.g. **il connaît, il paraît**, in the infinitive, and throughout the future and conditional (which take the infinitive minus the final -**e** as their stem), e.g. **je connaîtrai, ils paraîtront, je connaîtrais, ils paraîtraient**.

Complete the following sentences, by filling in the gaps with the appropriate form of the verb indicated, paying attention to use of the circumflex where necessary.

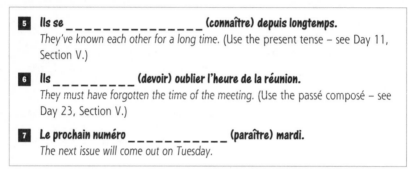

5 **Ils se _ _ _ _ _ _ _ _ _ _ _ _ _ _ _ _ (connaître) depuis longtemps.**
They've known each other for a long time. (Use the present tense – see Day 11, Section V.)

6 **Ils _ _ _ _ _ _ _ _ _ (devoir) oublier l'heure de la réunion.**
They must have forgotten the time of the meeting. (Use the passé composé – see Day 23, Section V.)

7 **Le prochain numéro _ _ _ _ _ _ _ _ _ _ _ (paraître) mardi.**
The next issue will come out on Tuesday.

iii) The cedilla

- Remember to use a cedilla under a '**c**' before '**a**', '**o**' or '**u**', if it is to be pronounced as [s] rather than [k], e.g. **ça**. Think of the vowels in the name 'Adolphus' if you have difficulty remembering which are the three problem vowels. You don't need a cedilla if the '**c**' is followed by '**e**' or '**i**', because then it is always pronounced [s], hence the difference between **cela** with no cedilla and the contracted form **ça** with a cedilla.
- Although you frequently see other accents omitted on capital letters, particularly the grave accent on capital '**A**', you must never omit a cedilla, if one is needed, from a capital '**C**', e.g. **Ça** at the beginning of a sentence.

Fill in the gaps in the following sentences, paying attention to the use of the cedilla where necessary.

8 **Il ne s'est _ _ _ _ _ _ _ _ _ (apercevoir) de rien.**
He didn't notice anything.

9 – 10 **A part _ _ _ _ _ _ , tout va bien.**
Apart from that, everything is fine.
(Give both the contracted and the full form for two marks.)

11 **Nous _ _ _ _ _ _ _ _ _ _ _ _ (recevoir) beaucoup.**
We do a lot of entertaining.

II Elision and word division

Note the following common problems:

- The articles (**le, la**) do not elide to **l'**, nor does **de** elide to **d'** before words beginning with an aspirate 'h'. For example:

le héros, de haute importance (see Day 7, Section I).

- **si** elides before **il(s)** to **s'il(s)**, but before **elle(s)** it does not, thus: **si elle(s)** (see Day 9, Section II).
- **que** elides to **qu'** before a vowel or inaspirate 'h', but **qui** never does (see Day 20, Section I). For example:

Voici le dossier qu'il cherchait.
[Here's the file he was looking for.]
Voilà le train qui arrive.
[Here's the train coming.]

- Note the difference between the pronouns **quelqu'un** (someone) and **chacun** (each one)**.** Avoid the common mistake of inventing the form ****chaqu'un**!
- Finally, note that **quelque chose** (something) is two separate words in French, but **quelquefois** (sometimes) – see Day 12, Section I – is one word.

Correct the errors in the following sentences. You should find only one error in each sentence.

---

12 **Chaqu'un a ses défauts.**
Everyone has their faults.

13 **Le bâtiment a 10 mètres d'hauteur.**
The building is 10 metres high.

14 **Ce qu'est affreux, c'est qu'il mange tout ce qu'il trouve à manger.**
What is awful is that he eats whatever food he can get.

15 **Je me demande si ils arriveront à temps et si elle pourra leur parler.**
I wonder whether they will arrive in time and if she will be able to speak to them.

16 **Il faudra dire quelquechose si elle nous voit.**
We'll have to say something if she sees us.

17 **C'est le hasard qu'a réuni les camarades.**
The friends were brought together by chance.

III   Capitalization

You need to remember the following cases where English uses a capital letter, but French uses a lower-case letter.

- For days of the week, months of the year and seasons, French uses a lower-case initial letter, e.g. **lundi**, **août**, **printemps**.
- Similarly, for streets, roads, squares, etc., French uses a lower-case letter, e.g. 20, rue de Vincennes.
- With titles accompanied by a proper name, French uses a lower-case letter, e.g. le docteur Bovary; le professeur Dupont; la reine Elisabeth. This applies even to monsieur, madame, mademoiselle Dumas, except when they are used in direct address, e.g. Mon cher Monsieur Dumas in a letter and when they are abbreviated to M., Mme, Mlle.
- In book titles, French does not use as many capital letters as you might expect. Typically, French capitalizes the first noun and anything which precedes it, but not anything which follows, e.g. *Les Fleurs du mal; La Femme rompue; Les Belles Images.*

Complete the gaps in the following sentences, making appropriate use of capitalization

18   Il a assisté aux Jeux Olympiques d'_ _ _ _ _ _ _ .
He went to the Winter Olympics.

19   Nous partons _ _ _ _ _ _ _ prochain.
We are leaving next Thursday.

20   Le _ _ _ _ _ _ Philippe II Auguste est né en 1165.
King Philip II Augustus was born in 1165.

21   Ils se marient en _ _ _ _ _ _ .
They are getting married in May.

22   Vous avez tous entendu parler du _ _ _ _ _ _ _ _ Pétain.
You have all heard of Marshal Pétain.

Correct the errors of capitalization in the following:

23   Il habite 34 Rue de Rennes.

24   Nous étudions *Les petits Enfants du siècle.*

25   Avez-vous vu *La Cantatrice Chauve?*

i)   Nationality, geographical origin

French uses a lower-case initial letter for adjectives of nationality/geographical origin, but a capital initial letter for nouns. For example:

> **un docteur français**
> [a French doctor]
> **un théâtre parisien**
> [a Parisian theatre]
> **Ce sont des Ecossais.**
> [They are Scots.]

Note particularly the difference between the following:

> Adjective: **Il est français.** – He is French
> Noun: **C'est un Français.** – He is a Frenchman.

It is a simpler matter when you are dealing with languages. French uses a lower-case initial letter for both nouns and adjectives. For example:

> **Elle parle italien.** She speaks Italian.
> **Ils ont écrit en langue anglaise.** They wrote in English.

Complete the gaps in the following sentences, making appropriate use of capitalization

---

26 *C'est un* _ _ _ _ _ _ _ _ *francophone.*
He is a French Canadian. (Which is noun and which is adjective here?)

27 *On m'a demandé de traduire cet article en* _ _ _ _ _ _ _ _ _ _ .
I've been asked to translate this article into German.

28 *J'aime bien la cuisine* _ _ _ _ _ _ _ _ _ _ _ _ _ .
I'm very fond of Greek food.

29 *Ces étudiants sont* _ _ _ _ _ _ _ _ _ _ .
These students are American.

30 *Ce sont des* _ _ _ _ _ _ _ _ _ _ _ _ _ _ _ .
They are Americans.

See for further information
Hawkins and Towell, Appendix
Judge and Healey, Chapter 20, §1.2.3
Byrne and Churchill, §§4–5, 9–12
Ferrar, Introduction: Spelling and Pronunciation

Revision: Use of articles, vocabulary and style

DAY 29

Today's exercises give you an opportunity to discover how much you have added to your active knowledge of French from the various points which you have covered in this book.

I Use of articles

Complete the following sentences with the appropriate article, **de +** article, or **de/d'** alone.

---

1 _ _ _ telles situations me font peur.
Such situations frighten me.

2 Il y a _ _ _ _ raisons d'espérer.
There are grounds for hope.

3 Le monde _ _ _ _ idées le fascine.
He is fascinated by the world of ideas.

4 Ils n'ont plus _ _ argent.
They have run out of money.

5 Ils ont besoin _ _ amis.
They need friends.

II Vocabulary

Complete the following sentences with an appropriate word/expression.

---

6 Elle s'était maquillée avec _ _ _ _ _ _ .
She had put her make-up on carefully.

7 Elle _ _ _ _ _ _ _ qu'elle n'a pas beaucoup travaillé.
She admits that she hasn't worked very hard.

8 La France _ _ _ _ _ _ _ _ _ _ deux millions de chômeurs. (Do not use avoir)
France has two million unemployed.

9 Il _ _ _ _ _ _ _ _ _ _ _ _ _ qu'il n'avait aucune intention d'écrire au client.
He retorted that he had no intention of writing to the customer.

10 Ils réalisent un _ _ _ _ _ _ _ _ d'affaires de 50 millions de francs par an.
They have a turnover of 50 million francs a year.

11 Il chante à tue-_ _ _ _ _ _ _.
He is singing very loudly.

12 Ils sont arrivés au mauvais _ _ _ _ _ _ _ _ _ _ _.
They arrived at the wrong time.

13 _ _ _ _ _ _ _ _ d'entre eux a reçu un cadeau.
Each of them received a present.

14 Les étudiants étaient peu _ _ _ _ _ _ _ _.
There weren't many students.

15 Les _ _ _ _ _ _ _ _ _ _ _ _ _ _ _ _ de Balzac représentent des espèces sociales.
Balzac's characters represent social types.

16 Je l'ai attendu _ _ _ _ _ _ _ _ _ une heure.
I waited for him for an hour.

17 Il a reçu les billets la _ _ _ _ _ _ _ _ _ de son départ.
He received the tickets the day before he left.

18 Je ne m'en suis jamais _ _ _ _ _ _ _ _ _.
I never suspected for a moment.

III   Style

Rewrite the following sentences, putting the underlined words at the beginning, and making any other necessary changes.

19 Les invités sont déjà arrivés <u>sans doute</u>.
The guests have doubtless already arrived.

20 Vous verrez <u>devant le restaurant universitaire</u> une longue queue d'étudiants.
You will see a long queue of students outside the university cafeteria.

21 Il est <u>tout seul</u> et il ne sait pas se débrouiller.
He is all on his own and can't manage.

22 J'ai prêté <u>mon vélo</u> à mon frère.
I've lent my bike to my brother.

23 Il a <u>peut-être</u> mal compris la question.
He perhaps misunderstood the question.

24 Je n'aurais jamais pensé à <u>partir en Italie</u>.
I'd never have thought of going off to Italy.

Correct the errors in the following sentences.

25 **Aussi les touristes sont tous partis.**
So the tourists have all left.

26 **Pourquoi est le train en retard?**
Why is the train late?

27 **«Je ne comprends pas» Susan a dit.**
'I don't understand,' Susan said.

28 **Elle s'est fait arrêtée.**
She got herself arrested.

29 **Çela se comprend.**
That's understandable.

30 **Est-ce que tu aimes la cuisine Grecque?**
Do you like Greek food?

After working your way through this book, you should have developed a more critical eye and an ability to spot the sort of slips which are liable to spoil your work. Put this to the test by working through these revision exercises which focus on the key points for which you should always check your own work:

- verb forms and tenses
- agreement of adjectives and past participles (first check the gender of the noun!)
- use of pronouns – personal and relative
- verb constructions (infinitive/present participle, passive, subjunctive, use of prepositions)

I   Verbs

Correct the errors in the following sentences, focusing your attention on verb forms and tenses.

1   Tout le monde connaissent Jean-Paul.
Everyone knows Jean-Paul.

2   Jean-Pierre et sa sœur étudent à l'université de Pau.
Jean-Pierre and his sister are studying at the University of Pau.

3   Quand il arrive vous devrez lui expliquer ce qui s'est passé.
When he arrives you'll have to tell him what has happened.

4   Les affaires reprendent un peu.
Business is picking up a bit.

5   Le bruit s'affaible.
The noise is getting fainter.

6   Je pouvais lui donner un coup de main, si j'avais le temps.
I could give him a hand if I had time.

7   Nous avons été travailler ici depuis six mois.
We have been working here for six months.

8   Il a mouru d'une crise cardiaque.
He died of a heart attack.

> **9**   **Si j'aurais le temps, je lirais tout le livre.**
> *If I had time, I would read the whole book.*
>
> **10**   **Il y avait été un grand scandale.**
> *There had been a big scandal.*

II   Agreements

Correct the errors in the following sentences, focusing your attention on the agreement of adjectives and past participles. You should find just one error in each sentence.

> **11**   **Touts les verres ont été cassés.**
> *All the glasses have been broken.*
>
> **12**   **Ils se sont aperçu de l'erreur surprenante.**
> *They noticed the surprising error.*
>
> **13**   **Elle s'est promise un nouvel appartement.**
> *She promised herself a new flat.*
>
> **14**   **Quels musées avez-vous visité?**
> *Which museums did you visit?*
>
> **15**   **Ils semblent déterminé à trouver quelque chose d'intéressant là-dedans.**
> *They seem determined to find something interesting in there.*
>
> **16**   **C'est l'une des attractions régionaux les plus connues.**
> *It's one of the best known regional attractions.*

III   Pronouns

Complete the following sentences by adding the appropriate personal or relative pronoun.

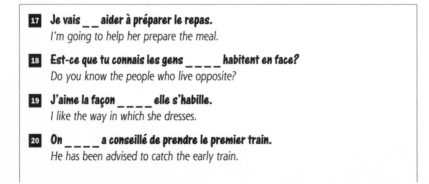

> **17**   **Je vais _ _ aider à préparer le repas.**
> *I'm going to help her prepare the meal.*
>
> **18**   **Est-ce que tu connais les gens _ _ _ _ habitent en face?**
> *Do you know the people who live opposite?*
>
> **19**   **J'aime la façon _ _ _ _ elle s'habille.**
> *I like the way in which she dresses.*
>
> **20**   **On _ _ _ _ a conseillé de prendre le premier train.**
> *He has been advised to catch the early train.*

21 **Nous ne nous _ _ _ souvenons pas.**
We don't remember it.

22 **Je ne _ _ avais pas pensé.**
I hadn't thought about it.

23 **Voici le texte _ _ _ _ j'ai fait référence.**
Here is the text to which I referred.

IV Verb constructions

Correct the errors in the following sentences, focusing on the verb construction. Look back at the work you did on days 14, 15, 21, 23 and 27 if in doubt.

24 **Il passe trop de temps en lisant.**
He spends too much time reading.

25 **Je vous préfère rester là.**
I prefer you to stay there.

26 **Nous les avons entendus rentrant.**
We heard them come back in.

27 **Elle a été demandée de rédiger le compte-rendu.**
She was asked to take the minutes.

28 **Ils s'asseyaient par terre.**
They were sitting on the floor.

29 **J'ai peur qu'il ne peut être trop tard!**
I fear it may be too late!

30 **Elle a approuvé de ma décision.**
She approved of my decision.

Progress Chart

Use this chart to track your daily progress. Use three colours: one for the vocabulary sections, one for grammar, and one for style. Then you will be able to see at a glance if you are weaker in one of the three areas and then make a special effort to compensate for that.

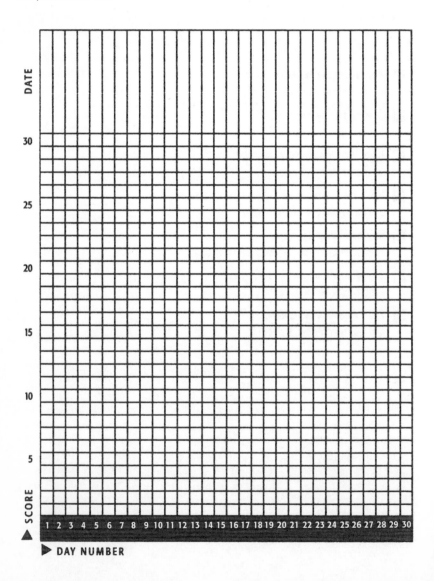

Answers to Exercises

Day 1
AGREEMENT OF VERB AND SUBJECT

1 J'attends
2 je pars
3 Elle veut
4 je ne peux pas
5 Elle ne rougit de rien
6 elle ne comprend pas.
7–8 Quand j'étais plus jeune, j'avais les cheveux longs.
9–10 Si j'avais pris le train de 9 heures j'y serais arrivé(e) à temps.
11 est
12 faisaient
13 va
14 sont
15 vont
16 sont
17 se rapprochent
18 allons
19 Il reste deux parts de gâteau.
20 Dans ces films il s'agit à peu près de la même histoire.
21 Le conseil municipal a décidé
22 La famille de Jean-Claude est
23 Tout le monde sait
24 Un groupe de musiciens répètent/répète (but the plural, répètent, is the more likely)
25 La moitié des étudiants se sont inscrits
26 La plupart des Hollandais parlent
27 60% des professeurs se déclarent satisfaits
28 La moitié de la classe a échoué.
29 Beaucoup de ses livres sont illisibles.
30 C'est moi qui fais la cuisine.

Day 2
REPORTING SPEECH

1 La plupart des députés considèrent (estiment/sont de l'avis/trouvent) que
2 Mon mari et moi avons fait remarquer/signalé
3 Beaucoup d'étudiants ont admis/avoué/reconnu
4 Le gouvernement annonça/déclara
5 Tout le monde considère (estime/est de l'avis/trouve)
6 Avant de conclure, il avait ajouté/précisé
7 Le ministre a expliqué/exposé les raisons
8 Elle répliqua (rétorqua/riposta)
9 Il constata (nota/observa)
10 Il nous a assurés (He assured us) qu'elle serait ravie de nous voir.
11 Il a constaté (He noted/observed that) qu'ils manquaient de personnel.
12 Ils ont avoué (They admitted that) qu'ils s'étaient trompés d'adresse.
13 Il signala (He pointed out) qu'elle serait déjà partie.
14 Elle avait rétorqué (She had retorted) qu'elle ne pouvait pas le supporter.
15 Elle a précisé (She added) qu'elle n'aurait pas le temps de lire l'article.
16 Le gouvernement affirma (The government claimed) que le taux du chômage avait baissé considérablement.
17 Il a expliqué (He explained) qu'ils auraient perdu la notion du temps.
18 Ils ont trouvé (They thought) qu'elle avait beaucoup maigri.
19 D'après sa secrétaire, il serait malade depuis trois jours.
20 Selon les témoins, on lui aurait donné de violents coups de pieds.
21 D'après la police, il s'agirait d'un incendie criminel.
22 A en croire le rapport, tout se serait bien passé.
23 Il a prétendu qu'il aurait été malade.
24 Il a prétendu que son frère lui aurait volé l'argent.

25 s'est-elle écriée.
26 précisa Sophie.
27 m'a demandé ma voisine.
28 s'est-elle demandé.
29 nous dit-il
30 observa le professeur

Day 3
THE PRESENT TENSE
1 Il présente
2 Ils étudient
3 Je vous remercie.
4 Tout le monde s'accorde
5 Je ne sais pas ce qui le travaille.
6 Ils mènent
7 Ils ne jettent jamais rien.
8 Elle emploie
9 Je préfère
10 nous nous plongeons
11 La ville s'agrandit.
12 Les gens ne choisissent pas
13 Les restaurants . . . envahissent les villes britanniques.
14 Elle se sent malade.
15 Ça ne répond pas.
16 Je te défends de sortir.
17 Ils s'attendent au pire.
18 Elle perçoit des droits d'auteur.
19 Les enfants meurent de faim.
20 Nous craignons une rechute.
21 Ces problèmes deviennent impossibles.
22 Les films hollywoodiens ne nous satisfont plus.
23 Ils apprennent leur métier.
24 Ils ne reçoivent pas assez d'argent.
25 Ils sont en train de rénover l'appartement.

26 Nous sommes en train de refaire tout son travail.
27 je recevais
28 je reçoive
29 je prenais
30 je prenne

Day 4
STATISTICS AND NUMBERS
1 le numéro un mondial
2–3 un numéro à trois chiffres.
4 Un grand nombre d'étudiants
5 Les chiffres officiels
6 un vieux numéro
7 le nombre de morts
8 a atteint un niveau sans précédent.
9 Le nombre des victimes s'élève à 18.
10 On compte 450 cas
11 est passé
12 a considérablement baissé
13 a augmenté
14 ont progressé
15 a augmenté
16 dont
17–18 Les femmes perçoivent en moyenne des salaires inférieurs
19–22 Le taux de chômage des femmes est supérieur à celui des hommes, soit 12% contre 8%.
23 La chute du franc
24 en baisse
25 1 750 000
26 15,5%
27 mille livres
28 L'an deux mille
29 deux millions de francs
30 des milliers

Day 5
ADJECTIVE AGREEMENTS
1 l'Union européenne
2 une démarche très légère
3 une vie très active
4 la cuisine grecque
5 est désespérée
6 Ce groupe est assez homogène
7 l'autre est plus mélangé.
8 un fol espoir
9 des fleurs artificielles
10 de beaux rêves
11–12 Toutes les diverses catégories
13–14 tous les directeurs régionaux
15 des huiles végétales
16 semblent capables
17 ceux qui étaient absents
18 Modèles féminins
19 des changements sociaux
20 des classes moyennes
21 les équilibres mondiaux
22 paraissent en effet bien fragiles
23 les conflits politiques sont multiples
24 l'un des plus beaux châteaux
25 maux de tête continuels
26 Seule, elle . . .
27 quelque chose d'intéressant
28 sont restés ensemble
29 On fait toujours les mêmes exercices
30 même les plus assidus

Day 6
ALTERNATIVES TO ADVERBS
1 sans ménagement
2 avec circonspection

3 sans pouvoir rien faire
4 sans distinction
5 Avec un peu de chance
6 par hasard
7 sur un ton très solennel
8 d'un ton sec
9 d'une façon/manière désastreuse
10 De façon inattendue
11 elle y voit clair
12 Vous avez deviné juste.
13 Ils parlent trop bas
14 C'est à peu près terminé.
15 Par la suite
16 en particulier
17 avant tout
18 au juste
19 Either: à pic Or: en flèche
20 dans son for intérieur
21 à bon compte
22 du bout des lèvres
23 Either: à contrecœur Or: de mauvais gré
24 A sa grande surprise
25 à brûle-pourpoint
26 Il est évident qu'il n'en sait rien.
27 Il est possible qu'ils arrivent plus tard.
28 Ses toiles sont d'une variété étonnante.
29 Elle a la conviction intime qu'il sera reçu.
30 Le sport est l'amour de sa vie.

Day 7
USE OF ARTICLES
1 Il faut mettre de l'huile dans les rouages.
2 La hiérarchie est tout à fait inaltérable.
3 C'est un produit de haute qualité.

4 Notre pays appartient au groupe des Sept.
5 L'authenticité des documents est mise en doute.
6 Je n'ai pas l'habitude de les voir le weekend.
7 Le hasard a voulu que je trouve la source des citations.
8 C'est l'unique voie qui y mène.
9–10 Cette influence des médias ne se limite pas au monde de la musique ou du cinéma.
11–12 La pollution de l'air est devenue un véritable problème de santé publique.
13 L'obsession de la qualité est une véritable manie chez les Japonais.
14–15 Avec les progrès de la mécanisation et de l'automatisation, les Français ont besoin de moins de calories.
16 Je pourrais vous en donner des dizaines d'exemples.
17 Je n'ai jamais eu de tels problèmes.
18 Ce sont des fanatiques.
19 La dépression peut aussi causer des problèmes physiques.
20 Ces étudiants sont des Ecossais.
21 Cela va provoquer des réactions.
22–3 Ils ont vécu de harengs et de pommes de terre pendant une semaine.
24 Il n'a pas le sens des responsabilités.

25 Il avait les yeux pleins de larmes.
26 L'histoire nous en fournit de nombreux exemples.
27 Ce sont des jeunes filles rangées.
28 Elle ne mange pas de pain.
29 Il a travaillé pendant de longues heures.
30 Il ne reste que des pommes.

Day 8 QUANTIFIERS
1 Bon nombre d'étudiants
2 de nombreuses années
3 nombre de témoins
4 énormément de cigares
5 Nous étions nombreux
6 Un très grand nombre d'étudiants
7 bien des années
8 pas mal d'amis
9 une quantité de touristes
10 J'ai peu de temps
11 Les étudiants sont peu nombreux.
12 L'eau est peu profonde.
13 la plus grosse part
14 le plus
15 une bonne partie
16 la majeure partie
17 la plus grande partie
18 presque tout le temps
19 autant de livres
20 Que de monde!
21 assez de place
22 le reste de mes affaires
23 Chacun d'entre vous
24 un certain effet
25 plusieurs heures
26 sur certains points
27 Un certain nombre
28 diverses explications
29 Certains d'entre eux
30 quelques mots

Day 9
USE OF TENSES WITH SI
1 C
2 Q
3 C
4 Q
5 C
6 Q
7 C
8 Si vous le voyez demain, dites-lui bonjour de ma part.
9 Je vous aurais invité si j'avais su que vous étiez là.
10 Si nous arrivons avant minuit, nous vous donnerons un coup de fil.
11 Elle a dit que s'il lui téléphonait elle raccrocherait tout de suite.
12 Elle a dit que si elle était fatiguée, elle ferait la sieste.
13 Si nous avons le temps, nous passerons les voir.
14 S'il avait lu ce texte, il aurait tout compris.
15 Si je pouvais vous aider, je le ferais volontiers.
16 Si elle avait plus d'argent, elle pourrait s'acheter une voiture.
17 Ils pourraient aller à Paris s'ils en avaient vraiment envie.
18 S'ils pouvaient partir, ils iraient aux Etats-Unis.
19 S'il a manqué le rendez-vous, il ne l'a pas fait exprès.
20 S'il est parti, je sais qu'il nous aura laissé un mot.
21 S'il partait, il essayerait de nous faire signe.

22 S'il y avait plus de pistes cyclables, nos enfants pourraient aller à l'école à bicyclette.
23 S'ils n'étaient pas aussi riches, prendrait-on au sérieux leurs arguments?
24 Si l'on pouvait trouver son dossier, peut-être pourrait-on résoudre le problème.
25 Sa situation changerait si elle était enceinte.
26 S'il n'y avait pas de discrimination, nous n'aurions pas besoin d'avoir une guerre des sexes.
27 Sans domicile fixe, il est difficile de trouver un emploi.
28 En cas d'incendie, brisez la glace.
29 En cas de panne, réfugiez-vous sur la bande d'arrêt d'urgence.
30 Ils ont dit qu'avec un peu de chance ils pourraient nous rejoindre plus tard.

Day 10
FALSE FRIENDS AND ANGLICIZED SPELLING
1 Les **problèmes** dont on discute sont très complexes.
2 Les **partis** politiques prennent position sur ce problème.
3 Ces plantes **exigent** des soins constants.
4 Il leur **pose** des questions trop difficiles.
5 Le **processus** de paix est très délicat.

6 Cet acteur sait vraiment se mettre dans la peau de son **personnage**.
7 C'est un accomplissement/exploit formidable.
8–9 **Finalement**, le train est arrivé avec deux heures de **retard**.
10 La police a entendu **le témoignage** de son voisin de palier.
11 **Le congrès** se déroulera à Montréal du 3 au 5 avril.
12 **Le changement** de stratégie les a beaucoup surpris.
13 Je le croyais dangereux, mais **en fait** c'est un bon conducteur.
14 Il a mené une campagne très **efficace**.
15 Il faut obtenir une note d'au moins 9 sur 20 pour **être reçu à** l'examen.
16 Il a travaillé huit heures d'affilée pour **achever** l'article.
17 parce que le **change** ne leur est pas favorable.
18 Il a gagné son **procès**.
19 Le cessez-le-feu est devenu **effectif** à minuit.
20 Vous pourriez **éventuellement** trouver ce conseil utile.
21 Je croyais que sa cousine était infirmière, mais **en fait** elle est médecin.
22 Je tiens à mettre en **évidence** le lien entre ces deux phénomènes.
23 Ces pages sont consacrées à une étude de **caractères**.

24 j'ai réussi à obtenir un **délai** de deux jours.

25 Prenons un ex**e**mple au hasard.

26 C'est un artiste sensatio**nn**el.

27 Il parle d'un ton très **a**gressif.

28 This sentence is correct. Compare English 'a**dd**ress' with the French a**d**resse.

29 Il s'est donné pour objecti**f** d'écrire deux mille mots par jour.

30 Ce livre s'adresse à un publi**c** jeune.

Day 11   PAST TENSES

1 Nous sommes retournés dans notre pays natal.

2 Qu'est-ce qu'il est devenu?

3 Il est survenu une difficulté inattendue.

4 Ils sont ressortis par la porte de derrière.

5 J'ai eu ce livre pour cinquante francs.

6 L'élection a été sans surprise.

7 Ils ont été contents de leur séjour.

8 Je me suis aperçu(e) d'une erreur.

9 Il a choisi de ne pas répondre.

10 Ces enfants ont appris à nager.

11 Ils se sont joints à la foule.

12 Il n'y a jamais eu de phénomène pareil.

13 S'il n'y avait pas eu de guerre

14 Il y a eu une explosion sociale.

15 Il ne savait pas qu'il y avait eu une catastrophe.

16 Elle ne savait pas qu'il était déjà arrivé.

17 Il se rendit compte qu'elle avait manqué le train.

18 Il l'invita à entrer et l'accompagna jusqu'au salon, où il avait été en train de travailler.

19 Pendant son absence à l'étranger, ses petits-enfants avaient beaucoup grandi.

20 Ils avaient bu trop de bière.

21 Ils ne viennent que d'emménager.

22 Ça fait quinze jours que je travaille à ce rapport.

23 Est-ce que vous savez depuis combien de temps il étudie à cette université?

24 Ils la connaissent depuis des années.

25 Est-ce que vous saviez qu'il habitait ici depuis si longtemps?

26 Elle ne venait que d'entendre la nouvelle quand elle m'a téléphoné.

27 Il avait fini son travail.

28 Elle ne savait pas qu'il était mort.

29 Il y a eu un incendie.

30 L'avion vient d'atterrir.

Day 12
EXPRESSIONS OF TIME

1 une fois par semaine.

2 pendant les heures du bureau.

3 Il faut du temps

4 A cette époque/En ce temps-là

5 à temps pour

6 Elle est parfois/quelquefois irritable.

7 C'est le bon moment

8 Elle est tout à la fois

9 dans les délais convenus.

10 depuis longtemps.

11 depuis deux ans

12 pendant quelques instants

13 Restez un moment.

14 pour le weekend.

15 Dans deux heures

16 en dix minutes.

17 dans une minute.

18 en un clin d'œil.

19 Les jours

20 en première année

21 toute une matinée de travail.

22 le matin.

23 en début de soirée.

24 Dans quelques années

25 dans les années soixante-dix

26 dans deux ans.

27 la veille au soir.

28 du jour au lendemain.

29 au lendemain de la guerre.

30 la veille de l'examen.

Day 13
AGREEMENT OF PAST PARTICIPLES

1 Les cambrioleurs ont forcé le patron à ouvrir la caisse.

2 Les écologistes nous ont avertis/averties de 'l'effet de serre'. Note that the agreement is with the preceding direct object, *nous*, not with the subject, *les écologistes*.

3 Je ne trouve pas les documents qu'elle m'a apportés ce matin.

4 Quelle idée de les avoir invités/invitées ce soir!

5 Le système nous a donné ce droit.

6 Cette date nous aurait bien convenu. (There is no agreement, because *nous* is an indirect object. The construction is *convenir à quelqu'un*).

7 Il les a persuadés d'assister à la réunion.

8 Le spectacle nous a beaucoup plu. (There is no agreement, because *nous* is an indirect object. The construction is *plaire à quelqu'un*).

9 Je les ai aidés à faire les mots croisés. (Note that the construction is *aider quelqu'un à faire quelque chose*. Students are sometimes confused by the occurrence of the preposition *à* before the following infinitive, but what matters is that there is no preposition before *quelqu'un*; in other words, *aider* takes a direct object.)

10 Il nous a téléphoné hier soir. (There is no agreement, because *nous* is an indirect object. The construction is *téléphoner à quelqu'un*.)

11 La concurrence est devenue intense.

12 Le Président et le Premier Ministre sont parvenus à un accord.

13 Nous sommes repartis sur de nouvelles bases.

14 Elle s'est lavé les cheveux.

15 Elle s'est promis un weekend à Londres.

16 Elles se sont servies les premières.

17 Elle s'est foulé la cheville.

18 Ils se sont serré la main.

19 Ils se sont aidés à faire leurs devoirs. (See the note to number 9 above.)

20 Elles se sont promis de garder le secret.

21 Ils se sont écrit tous les jours.

22 Ils se sont fait beaucoup de mal.

23 Quand est-ce qu'elle s'est mise à tousser?

24 Ils se sont posé la même question.

25 Les femmes se sont battues pour gagner le droit de vote.

26 Elle s'est moquée de lui.

27 Ils se sont envoyé leurs vœux pour la nouvelle année.

28 Les restrictions qu'ils se sont imposées sont à faire peur.

29–30 Les souvenirs qu'elle s'est rappelés l'ont beaucoup émue.

Day 14
PRONOMINAL VERBS

1 Tu devrais te reposer.

2 Je m'occupe de vous tout de suite.

3 Nous nous passerons d'elle.

4 Est-ce que vous vous souvenez de lui?

5 Ils se sont gardés de révéler le résultat.

6 Je dois m'occuper des enfants

7 Nous aurions dû nous douter qu'il y aurait un problème.

8 Elle s'est rendue à Londres en avion.

9 Vous vous moquez de moi.

10 Je ne peux pas me passer de mon diction- naire.

11 les camions doivent s'arrêter

12 Mes pensées se sont tournées vers ma famille.

13 J'ai tourné les yeux vers lui.

14 Je n'arrive pas à me concentrer.

15 Nous nous sommes séparés à la gare.

16 Elle se sent libre de partir

17 ça sent mauvais

18 Ils se sentent bien mieux maintenant.

19 Est-ce que vous vous sentez nerveux?

20 L'enfant était blotti

21 Elle s'est agenouillée

22 Elle était agenouillée

23 La bicyclette était appuyée

24 Elle était assise

25 Elle était allongée/couchée/éten- due

26 Nous devons nous rendre compte

27 Je vais me concentrer

28 La résurgence du nationalisme pose un grand problème.

29 Un enfant doit se sentir en sécurité.
30 elle etait assise à lire.

Day 15
THE PASSIVE

1 Nos grands-parents n'ont pas été **exposés** à ces dangers.
2 Plusieurs de ses romans ont **été adaptés** pour le cinéma.
3 Sans l'aide de la communauté internationale, certaines minorités ethniques risquent d'être complètement **anéanties**.
4 Cette pièce a été **créée** à la Comédie Française.
5 Mes frais de déplacement sont payés par mon chef.
6 Ces enfants n'auraient jamais été abandonnés par leur mère.
7 La famille a été désunie par cette crise.
8 Les enfants seront gardés par la jeune fille au pair.
9 Des élections avaient été organisées par les étudiants.
10 Que les critiques soient désarmés par le spectacle!
11 L'équipe risque d'être épuisée par cette aventure.
12 Son absence pourrait être expliquée par ce fait.
13 Ce bâtiment a été/fut conçu par un architecte célèbre.

14 Nous avons été invités à dîner hier par nos nouveaux voisins.
15 Elle a été frappée/étonnée d'entendre qu'il avait réussi à son examen.
16 Le rédacteur était très bien vu de ses collègues.
17 No.
18 Yes.
19 No.
20 No.
21 On m'a conseillé de chercher ailleurs.
22 On m'a promis un nouveau poste.
23 On m'a dit qu'il ne veut plus me voir.
24 Nous nous sommes vu offrir un nouvel appartement par le propriétaire.
25 Nous nous sommes vu refuser l'accès du bâtiment.
26 Elle s'est vu/entendu conseiller de partir dès que possible.
27 Tout cela se passe dans un pays qui s'est vu **diviser** en deux états après la deuxième guerre mondiale.
28 On leur a donné le choix de rester en Algérie ou de retourner en France. (Also possible: Ils se sont vu donner le choix de rester en Algérie ou de retourner en France.)
29 On lui a demandé de payer en avance. (Also possible: Il s'est vu/entendu demander de payer en avance.)
30 On m'a montré le nouveau bâtiment. (Also possible: Je me suis vu

montrer le nouveau bâtiment.)

Day 16
ALTERNATIVES TO THE PASSIVE

1 No, because I was blinded by a specified agent, the sun.
2 Yes.
3 Yes.
4 No, because the agent, lightning, is specified.
5 Son patron lui a offert une augmentation (de salaire).
6 Son père lui a appris à conduire.
7 Le champagne se boit frais.
8 Les fraises se vendaient à trente francs le kilo.
9 Le centre-ville s'est transformé.
10 Enfin la porte s'ouvrit.
11 Yes.
12 No (because the agent, 'the locals', is expressed).
13 No (because the subject is a person; *elle s'est emprisonnée* would mean 'she imprisoned herself').
14 Yes.
15 Il s'est fait/laissé harceler par les manifestants.
16 Elle s'est laissé tromper par son mari.
17 Si tu ne fais pas attention, tu vas te faire piquer.
18 Il s'est vu nommer à Aix.
19 Elle s'est vu promouvoir du rang de secrétaire.

20 L'équipe se verra reléguer dans la division inférieure.
21 Depuis son licenciement, il est très déprimé.
22 Ils aimeraient voir l'abolition de ces règles.
23 Après la dissolution du parlement, il y avait une grande confusion.
24 Ce rapport est à terminer aujourd'hui.
25 Son devoir était à entièrement revoir.
26 Ces papiers sont à jeter.
27 Elle s'est fait (or Elle se fit) comprendre tant bien que mal.
28 Ce n'est pas une femme avec qui l'on badine!
29 Cela ne s'écrit jamais.
30 Nous attendons la livraison des marchandises.

Day 17
PERSONAL PRONOUNS
1 Elle aurait dû arriver au siège de l'entreprise ce matin.
2 Elles ne savent pas pourquoi.
3 elles étaient sur mon bureau
4 Ils ont l'intention d'organiser une sortie ensemble.
5 Ils datent du quatorzième siècle.
6 On leur offre des places gratuites.
7 Ce cadeau lui a beaucoup plu.
8 Ses parents l'ont encouragé à chercher un travail à l'étranger.

9 Ce travail leur a donné beaucoup de soucis.
10 de leur acheter des baskets
11 leurs parents pouvaient les aider
12 Ce qui les ennuie
13–14 Il leur a téléphoné des Etats-Unis pour avoir de leurs nouvelles.
15 Avez-vous les moyens de les payer?
16 Je suis arrivé à le configurer.
17 Il a persuadé ses parents de le payer.
18 Je vais aider ma sœur à les déballer.
19 Je n'en ai pas.
20 Nous pouvons nous en passer.
21 Elle s'en sert maintenant.
22 Ils en ont besoin demain.
23 qui préfèrent s'y adhérer.
24 Elle y a signé son nom.
25 Est-ce que tu y as pensé?
26 Je ne sais pas ce que vous en pensez.
27 Je te demande d'y faire très attention.
28 J'y suis allé.
29 Je n'ai aucune envie d'y aller.
30 nous en serions ravis.

Day 18   THE NEGATIVE
1 Rien ne va changer.
2 Personne ne sait ce qui se passe.
3 Je ne les connais ni l'un ni l'autre.
4 Elle n'a aucune envie de s'installer à Paris.

5 Ni elle ni moi ne connaissons la ville.
6 Jamais, même dans ses rêves les plus fous, elle n'avait imaginé qu'elle allait gagner.
7 Il n'y a plus rien à faire ici.
8 Il n'y a jamais personne pour résoudre le problème.
9 Je ne connais plus personne dans le quartier.
10 N'avez-vous rien vu?
11 Elle ne l'a jamais aimé.
12 N'avez-vous vu personne?
13 On n'en a trouvé nulle part.
14 Elle n'avait étudié aucun dossier.
15 Je lui ai demandé de ne pas parler à Sandrine.
16 Je lui ai demandé de ne parler à personne.
17 Nous préférons ne pas dîner avant vingt heures.
18 Il a envie de ne rien faire.
19 Une mère ne peut travailler que si elle a l'aide et le soutien de sa famille.
20 Ce n'est que lui qui s'occupe du jardin.
21 On ne trouve ces plantes qu'à basse altitude.
22 On ne trouve que ces plantes à haute altitude.
23 Elle ne réussit ses examens qu'après de longues heures de préparation.
24 Ils n'adorent pas les enfants.
25 Elle n'a pas fait d'erreur.

26 Il ne reste pas de chambres simples.

27 Je n'ai rien acheté.

28 Elle ne comprend pas du tout ce qu'il raconte.

29 Personne ne me l'a jamais expliqué.

30 Je leur avais demandé de ne pas téléphoner après minuit.

Day 19
INVERSION OF VERB AND SUBJECT

1 Est-ce que cet ingrédient est absolument essentiel?

2 Est-ce que ce cours est intéressant?

3 Pourquoi existe-**t**-elle?

4 Complex inversion is necessary after *pourquoi*: Pourquoi les contribuables britanniques devraient-ils payer une telle chose?

5 Avez-vous eu de ses nouvelles?

6 Vous a-t-elle téléphoné?

7 Le courrier est-il arrivé?

8 Pourquoi le livre n'est-il pas paru?

9 Qu'en pensent les étudiants?

10 De quoi s'agit-il dans le film?

11 Comment le gouvernement va-t-il régler l'affaire?

12 Either simple or complex inversion is possible here: Où se passe l'action? or Où l'action se passe-t-elle?

13 «Où avez-vous trouvé ces documents?» demanda le ministre.

14 «Entrez», cria-t-elle.

15 Sans doute les écologistes ont-ils raison.

16 Du moins est-elle restée dans les délais.

17 A peine était-il arrivé qu'il pensait déjà à repartir.

18 Peut-être manquent-ils de personnel.

19 De là découlent tous vos problèmes.

20 Bientôt arriva l'automne, morne et pluvieux.

21 Ensuite survint un nouvel obstacle.

22 Je ne comprends pas ce que dit mon professeur.

23 La gauche dénonce ces mesures dont sont victimes les individus les plus faibles.

24 Ce sont des individus que ne protège aucune organisation.

25 Il est moins courageux que ne le pensent ses soldats.

26 Quelles que soient les difficultés, nous ne pouvons pas abandonner.

27 Au rythme où vont les choses, nous n'en finirons jamais.

28 Voilà le bâtiment d'où s'élève de la fumée.

29 Le chien gémit toujours, quoiqu'ait cessé tout bruit de pas.

30 Tant que vivait son époux, elle était restée à Paris.

Day 20
RELATIVE PRONOUNS

1 Je n'en reviens pas des progrès **qu'**il a faits.

2 Est-ce que tu as vu la lettre **qui** est arrivée ce matin?

3 Il va enfin terminer la dissertation **qui** le préoccupe depuis si longtemps.

4 Voulez-vous accueillir les clients **qui** attendent dehors?

5 Le repas **qu'**elle avait préparé était délicieux.

6 Je ne supporte pas la façon **dont** il parle.

7 J'ai oublié le dossier **dont** j'ai besoin.

8 C'est un film **que** je me rappellerai toujours. C'est un film **dont** je me souviendrai toujours.

9 C'est un ancien étudiant **dont j'ai oublié le nom**.

10 Voilà le spécialiste **dont je vous ai donné l'adresse**.

11 La maison contre **laquelle** le camion s'est heurté a été déclarée dangereuse.

12 L'enfant après **qui** il court est le fils de ses voisins.

13 Ce sont des termes **auxquels** il ne pourra jamais consentir.

14 Je ne pourrais pas supporter les odeurs de cuisine au milieu **desquelles** vous travaillez.

15 Ce film passe au cinéma près **duquel** il habite.

16 La pièce **où** elle travaille est très mal éclairée.

17 On sonna à la porte au moment **où** je commençais à préparer le repas.

18 Le jour **où** ils sont partis en vacances il a fait très beau.

19 Je l'ai rencontré un jour **que** je faisais mes courses.

20 Je n'aime pas la ville **où** ils se sont installés.

21 J'ai fait tout **ce que** je peux pour elle.

22 Elle m'a écrit une longue lettre, **ce qui** m'a beaucoup surpris.

23 Elle lui a écrit une lettre **qui** l'a fait rire.

24 Est-ce que vous avez tout **ce dont** vous avez besoin?

25 **Ce que** je voudrais vraiment faire ce soir, c'est aller au cinéma.

26 C'est une question **dont** les cinéphiles européens se préoccupent beaucoup.

27 Reste à savoir si les cinéastes réussiront à obtenir l'argent **dont** ils ont besoin.

28 Je vais expliquer les raisons **pour lesquelles** je ne suis pas partisan de cette affirmation préliminaire.

29 Cette guerre des sexes remonte à l'époque **où** les femmes ont soudain découvert leur liberté sexuelle.

30 **Ce qu'**il y a de certain, c'est qu'il n'y arrivera jamais.

Day 21
THE INFINITIVE AND PRESENT PARTICIPLE

1 Il finira par se blesser.

2 C'est une manière de voir les choses.

3 Avant de partir, ils ont coupé le gaz.

4 Je les ai regardés jouer au tennis.

5 Elle a le don de m'énerver.

6 Ils ont passé trois heures à se débattre avec leurs devoirs.

7 Est-il possible de contracter ce virus en mangeant du bœuf?

8 La famille passe la soirée à regarder la télévision.

9 Après avoir lu son rapport, je comprends mieux la situation.

10 Après avoir terminé mon travail, je suis allé me promener dans le parc.

11 Après être tombé de cheval, elle a passé une semaine à l'hôpital.

12 C'est l'idéologie dominante.

13 C'est une collection rassemblant des objets des quatre coins du monde.

14 Je ne trouve pas ses idées très convaincantes.

15 On apprend en vieillissant.

16 Sachant qu'il est très sérieux, je suis sûr qu'il va réussir.

17 En attendant son arrivée, je vais ranger la chambre.

18 En arrivant à Paris, nous avons téléphoné à nos amis.

19 De l'autre côté de la rue il y avait une file d'étudiants attendant l'ouverture de la cafétéria.

20 Tout en voulant assister au congrès, je ne peux vraiment pas me le permettre.

21 Tout en tricotant, elle nous racontait des histoires.

22 Dès qu'il a vu la police, il est parti en courant.

23 Il s'est avancé en boitant vers la porte.

24 J'ai monté l'escalier en rampant.

25 Je préfère travailler tout(e) seul(e).

26 Je préfère qu'ils travaillent tous seuls.

27 Elle veut que nous passions les voir la semaine prochaine.

28 Je voudrais passer les voir la semaine prochaine.

29 Est-il vraiment nécessaire que vous alliez à Londres?

30 Il est essentiel/indispensable de réviser les épreuves avec beaucoup de soin.

Day 22
LOGICAL CONNECTORS

1 Je voudrais tout d'abord vous remercier

2 Dans un premier temps

3 Ensuite nous passerons

4 Dans un dernier temps

5 Tout compte fait

6 Pour conclure; pour terminer

7 Ce type d'argument est aussi difficile à prouver qu'à réfuter.

8 La piscine est ouverte été comme hiver.

9 Les employés sont surmenés, et qui plus est, sous-payés; Les employés sont surmenés, et plus important encore, sous-payés; Les employés sont non seulement surmenés, mais aussi sous-payés.

10 Ce problème touche les jeunes aussi bien que les vieux; Ce problème touche non seulement les jeunes, mais aussi les vieux.

11 C'est le symbole à la fois de la vie et de l'espoir; C'est le symbole non seulement de la vie, mais aussi de l'espoir.

12 Les hommes politiques, de droite comme de gauche; Les hommes politiques, non seulement de droite, mais aussi de gauche

13 L'accusé n'a pas répondu, d'où l'on peut tirer ses propres conclusions.

14 Elle a beaucoup travaillé, aussi a-t-elle réussi.

15 c'est pourquoi je vous en envoie un double.

16 Ainsi, vous refusez de m'aider?

17 puisque cela remettrait en question

18 Attendu que/Etant donné que vous vous êtes excusé

19 Vu qu'il est déjà dix-huit heures

20 Dès lors que

21 Certes, l'examen est difficile, mais pas impossible; L'examen est difficile, certes, mais pas impossible; Bien que l'examen soit difficile, il n'est pas impossible.

22 Il a été très gentil, j'ai un reproche à lui faire cependant; Il a été très gentil, et néanmoins j'ai un reproche à lui faire; Il a été très gentil, j'ai toutefois un reproche à lui faire; Bien qu'il ait été très gentil, j'ai un reproche à lui faire.

23 Certes, ce travail prend du temps, mais il n'est pas difficile; Ce travail prend du temps, certes, mais il n'est pas difficile; Bien que ce travail prenne du temps, il n'est pas difficile; Ce travail prend du temps, pourtant/toutefois/cependant il n'est pas difficile.

24 Bien qu'il le sache, il ne veut pas l'admettre; Il le sait, pourtant il ne veut pas l'admettre.

25 En revanche/Par contre, rares sont les élus

26 Le produit national brut du Japon augmente d'année en année tandis que/alors que celui de la Grande-Bretagne est constamment en baisse; Le produit national brut du Japon augmente d'année en année. En revanche/Par contre celui de la Grande-Bretagne est constamment en baisse; Contrairement au produit national brut du Japon qui augmente d'année en année, celui de la Grande-Bretagne est constamment en baisse.

27 She says she spent the evening in the library, and yet (opposition) no one saw her there.

28 We looked up all the articles but couldn't find the necessary reference. So (concluding an argument) we had to admit defeat.

29 We should have checked the papers, but (opposition) no-one thought of it.

30 I had already written an essay on the foreign policy of de Gaulle, and it just so happened (introducing a new element) that that was the first question on the paper.

Day 23   MODAL VERBS

1 J'irais en France

2 Elle ne veut pas ranger sa chambre.

3 Elle passait des heures

4 Il ne voulait rien faire or il n'a rien voulu faire

5 Les enfants resteront

6 Que devrais-je faire?

7 S'ils téléphonent

8 Je ne sais pas si je devrais en parler

9 je prendrais ma retraite

10 Je n'aurais pas dû quitter la maison.

11 j'aurais préparé le repas.

12 Vous n'auriez pas dû rester aussi longtemps.

13 Cela pourrait avoir beaucoup de succès.

14 Je pourrais vous voir

15 Pourrais-je laisser un message?

16 Elle n'a pas pu manger

17 Bien qu'il en ait besoin

18 Vous pouvez faire

19 quoi qu'il arrive.

20 Ce médicament peut provoquer des réactions de somnolence.

21 Je crains qu'il ne fasse une bêtise.

22 Cela pourrait être difficile.

23 je pouvais partir

24 de peur qu'il ne parle.

25 Il doit déjà le savoir.

26 Il a dû partir hier.

27 Nous devons rester

28 Ils ont dû aller à l'hôpital.

29 Je vois la mer

30 Je sentais une odeur de brûlé.

Day 24
SENTENCE OPENINGS

1 Sur la place on trouve un petit marché.

2 Ce jour-là les Lyonnais ont illuminé leurs balcons de milliers de lampions.

3 Devant le restaurant on voit un étalage alléchant de fruits de mer.

4 Hier matin le Premier Ministre a exposé son programme.

5 A chaque coin de rue il y a des vendeurs de marrons chauds.

6 Loin de sa famille elle se laisse dépérir.

7 Fatiguée, elle s'arrêta.

8 Appelée durant la Révolution «Port La Montagne», Toulon mérite bien cette dénomination.

9 Toute seule, elle sombre dans le désespoir.

10 Isolées et sauvages, ces îles offrent un paysage magnifique.

11 De style flamboyant, le clocher date du seizième siècle.

12 Ville accueillante et dynamique, Montpellier s'enorgueillit de nombreuses attractions touristiques.

13 Chef-d'œuvre d'architecture gothique, la Sainte-Chapelle est située dans l'enceinte du Palais de Justice.

14 Ville historique, Dijon nous a légué un certain nombre de jardins anciens.

15 Grand centre industriel, Rouen est aussi un important centre commercial aux magasins fascinants.

16 Suite à l'article d'hier, j'ai écrit au rédacteur.

17 Sans elle il ne peut rien faire.

18 En dépit de mes conseils elle a démissionné.

19 A force de patience ils ont réussi.

20 Grâce à elle je suis parvenu à mon but.

21 Afin de ne pas vous déranger il a baissé le volume.

22 Après l'avoir lu j'ai changé d'avis.

23 Avant de rédiger sa réponse elle a relu la lettre.

24 Alors même qu'il le pourrait, il ne veut pas poursuivre ses études.

25 Tandis que nous travaillons, elle s'amuse.

26 Bien que les examens approchent, elle ne travaille pas.

27 De peur qu'il n'y ait une explosion, il a fermé le gaz.

28 Bien que de faibles dimensions, comme toutes les cathédrales bretonnes, la cathédrale Saint-Corentin domine le paysage quimpérois.

29 Bien que peu imposante, l'église a une histoire mouvementée.

30 Bien que très jeune, il sait s'imposer.

Day 25   CONJUNCTIONS

1 P

2 C

3 C

4 P

5 C

6 C

7 Quand j'aurai fini

8 dès que vous arriverez.

9 Pendant que j'attendrai

10 aussitôt que je saurai les résultats.

11 lorsqu'elle le verrait

12 dès qu'elle serait prête.

13 Depuis qu'elle était aveugle

14 Depuis qu'il habite à Paris

15 sans que je les voie

16 Avant que je ne leur écrive

17 Dès qu'il rentrera

18 Bien que je le connaisse

19 à moins que tu ne veuilles l'agacer.

20 A mesure qu'elle grandissait

21 A condition que tu fasses la vaisselle

22 pour qu'elle sache

23 de sorte que je ne peux pas

24 Une fois qu'ils se sont expliqués

25 de peur qu'elle ne soit prise de panique.

26 The student has used the preposition *après* instead of the conjunction *après que* to introduce a subordinate clause, but given that the subject of the subordinate clause is the same as the subject of the main clause, it would be more natural in French to use *après* followed by a perfect infinitive, i.e. Une femme peut retourner à son travail après avoir eu un enfant.

27 A moins d'avoir

28 afin d'aller

29 à condition de pouvoir

30 Avant de me décider

Day 26
HIGHLIGHTING AND EMPHASIS

1 Mon amie, je l'admire parce qu'elle est pleine d'entrain.

2 Notre appartement, nous l'avons loué à un collègue.

3 Ces copies, je vais les corriger ce soir.

4 Aller au théâtre, je n'en ai pas le temps.

5 Apprendre le russe, elle y tient beaucoup.

6 Retourner en Amérique, ils en ont vraiment envie.

7 Il est mort, son père.

8 Il en a pris, du poids.

9 Il l'a rendue hier, sa dissertation.

10 Ils sont enquiquinants, ces changements.

11 Vous en avez, des problèmes.

12 Elle se fait respecter, cette femme.

13 Eux, ils ne travaillent pas assez. (Also possible: Ils ne travaillent pas assez, eux.)

14 Mon amie, elle, ne veut pas sortir ce soir.

15 Moi, je ne comprends pas cet article. (Also possible: Je ne comprends pas cet article, moi. Or: Je ne comprends pas, moi, cet article.)

16 Vous, vous prenez tout de travers. (Also possible: Vous prenez tout de travers, vous.)

17 Nos voisins, eux, ne supportent pas le bruit.

18 Lui, il adore le sport. (Also possible: Il adore le sport, lui.)

19 Ce sont eux qui ont tenu parole.

20 Ce sont les étudiants qui ont tout organisé.

21 C'est à Marie-Hélène que l'on a offert le poste.

22 Ce n'est pas demain que je dois passer mon examen.

23 C'est à l'ouest qu'il fera du soleil.

24 Ce sont eux que j'ai vus hier.

25 Ce qui m'intéresse surtout, c'est la poésie contemporaine.

26 Ce que je ne supporte pas, c'est son insolence.

27 Ce qui le fatiguait de plus en plus, c'était faire la navette entre Paris et Lyon.

28 Ce qu'elle aimait surtout, c'était flâner dans le quartier latin.

29 Ce dont vous aurez besoin, c'est d'un parapluie.

30 Ce qu'elle déteste, c'est faire la cuisine.

Day 27
VERB CONSTRUCTIONS

1 Ils partent pour Paris demain.

2 Il a dû s'arrêter

3 Les locataires ont laissé l'appartement dans un état épouvantable.

4 Nous partons de chez nous

5 Ils vont quitter l'école

6 Il a payé cher sa réussite.

7 Je l'ai regardé fixement.

8 Je vais le lui demander.

9 Nous attendons le bus

10 Ce projet de loi vise les chômeurs.

11 Je vais lui téléphoner

12 Ce film leur a beaucoup plu.

13 Cette crème résiste à l'eau.

14 Je n'y avais pas pensé.

15 Il n'obéit pas aux règles.

16 Est-ce que vous en avez besoin?

17 Je me souviens très bien d'eux.

18 Il en doute.

19 La maison dont elle a hérité

20 Nous avons changé d'adresse.

21 Je t'en remercie.

22 De quoi vit-elle?

23 Il joue très bien de la flûte.

24 Qu'est-ce que tu en penses?

25 Maintenant que j'y pense

26 Il faut penser à votre carrière!

27 Ils jouent aux échecs.

28 L'examen consiste en deux épreuves.

29 Elle s'est fâchée contre lui

30 Nous l'avons vu entrer dans la maison

Day 28
ACCENTS. ELISION AND CAPITALIZATION

1 espérances.

2 Où

3 à

4 Ça y est

5 Ils se connaissent

6 Ils ont dû

7 Le prochain numéro paraîtra

8 Il ne s'est aperçu de rien.

9–10 A part cela/ça

11 Nous recevons beaucoup.

12 Chacun a ses défauts.

13 de hauteur

14 Ce qui est affreux

15 Je me demande s'ils arriveront

16 Il faudra dire quelque chose

17 C'est le hasard qui a réuni les camarades.

18 Jeux Olympiques d'hiver

19 jeudi prochain

20 Le roi Philippe II Auguste

21 en mai

22 Vous avez tous entendu parler du maréchal Pétain.

23 34 rue de Rennes

24 *Les Petits Enfants du siècle*

25 *La Cantatrice chauve*

26 C'est un Canadien francophone.

27 en allemand

28 la cuisine grecque

29 Ces étudiants sont américains.

30 Ce sont des Américains.

Day 29
USE OF ARTICLES, VOCABULARY AND STYLE

1 De telles situations

2 Il y a des raisons d'espérer.

3 Le monde des idées le fascine.

4 Ils n'ont plus d'argent.

5 Ils ont besoin d'amis.

6 avec soin

7 Elle admet/avoue/reconnaît

8 La France compte deux millions de chômeurs.

9 Il a répliqué/rétorqué/riposté

10 un chiffre d'affaires

11 à tue-tête

12 au mauvais moment

13 Chacun d'entre eux

14 peu nombreux

15 Les personnages de Balzac

16 pendant une heure

17 la veille de son départ

18 Je ne m'en suis jamais douté.

19 Sans doute les invités sont-ils déjà arrivés.

20 Devant le restaurant universitaire vous verrez une longue queue d'étudiants.

21 Tout seul, il ne sait pas se débrouiller.

22 Mon vélo, je l'ai prêté à mon frère.

23 Peut-être a-t-il mal compris la question (or, more colloquially, Peut-être qu'il a mal compris la question).

24 Partir en Italie, je n'y aurais jamais pensé.

25 Aussi les touristes sont-ils tous partis.

26 Pourquoi le train est-il en retard? (or Pourquoi est-ce que le train est en retard?)

27 «Je ne comprends pas» a dit Susan.

28 Elle s'est fait arrêter.

29 Cela (no cedilla on the 'C') se comprend.

30 Est-ce que tu aimes la cuisine grecque?

Day 30   KEY POINTS

1 Tout le monde connaît (third-person singular verb) Jean-Paul.

2 Jean-Pierre et sa sœur étud**i**ent à l'université de Pau.

3 Quand il arrivera (future tense after **quand** when the verb in the main clause is in the future).

4 Les affaires repre**nn**ent un peu.

5 Le bruit s'affaib**lit**.

6 Je pourrais lui donner un coup de main

7 Nous travaillons ici depuis six mois. (Use the present tense with *depuis* to translate 'have been working'.)

8 Il est mort

9 Si j'avais le temps

10 Il y avait **eu** un grand scandale.

11 **Tous** les verres ont été cassés.

12 Ils se sont aperçu**s** de l'erreur surprenante.

13 Elle s'est **promis** un nouvel appartement. (The past participle does not agree with the reflexive pronoun, because **se** is an indirect object: *on promet quelque chose à quelqu'un*.)

14 Quels musées avez-vous **visités**? (The past participle agrees with the preceding direct object, *musées*.)

15 Ils semblent dét**é**rminé**s**

16 C'est l'une des attractions **régionales** (This is the regular feminine plural form of the adjective.)

17 Je vais l'aider

18 Est-ce que tu connais les gens qui habitent en face?

19 J'aime la façon dont elle s'habille.

20 On lui a conseillé de prendre le premier train.

21 Nous ne nous en souvenons pas. (*se souvenir de quelque chose*)

22 Je n'y avais pas pensé. (*penser à quelque chose*)

23 Voici le texte auquel j'ai fait référence.

24 Il passe trop de temps à lire.

25 Je préfère que vous restiez là.

26 Nous les avons entendus rentrer.

27 On lui a demandé de rédiger le compte-rendu.

28 Ils étaient assis par terre.

29 J'ai peur qu'il ne soit trop tard!

30 Elle a approuvé ma décision.

Bibliography

Byrne, L.S.R. and Churchill, E.L., revised by G. Price, 1993, 4th edition. *A Comprehensive French Grammar.* Oxford: Blackwell.

Ferrar, H. 1982, 2nd edition. *A French Reference Grammar.* Oxford: Oxford University Press.

Hawkins, R. and Towell, R. 2001, 2nd edition. *French Grammar and Usage.* London: Arnold and Lincolnwood, Illinois: NTC Publishing Group.

Jubb, M.A. and Rouxeville, A. 1998. *French Grammar in Context: Analysis and Practice.* London: Arnold and Lincolnwood, Illinois: NTC Publishing Group.

Judge, A. and Healey, F. 1997, ninth impression: *A Reference Grammar of Modern French.* London: Arnold and Lincolnwood, Illinois: NTC Publishing Group.

Reference grammars cited in the text are cited in date order of publication, with the most recent first.

Index

This index uses roman type to refer to explanatory coverage and practice of each point in *Upgrade*. Italics are used for references to pages where a point arises incidentally, and is not the main focus of the explanation or exercise. This index does not refer you to the answer section except where an explanation appears there.